Praise for No Arms, No Legs, No Problem

"Bob Lujano is an amazing guy. His story is equal parts heartwarming, horrifying, amazing and inspiring. Everyone should read it."

–Lou Anders, Hugo award winner

"Bob Lujano is a remarkable man. He lived through intense abuse, neglect and prejudice long *before* he contracted the infection that would take his arms and legs. Most people couldn't suffer through half his struggles without succumbing to despair. But Bob's faith, hope, and love are the secret to a victorious and beautiful life. His book brought me to tears I'm privileged to call him a friend."

–David Anders, Ph.D. host of *EWTN Open Line*

"Move over self-pity, there's a new voice in town. For everyone who views people with disabilities as incapacitated or impaired, this book will take your preconceived ideas, put them in a blender with champagne, and raise a glass to all life has to offer."

–Lori Nichols, author-illustrator of the award-winning picture book *Maple*

"Perseverance, discipline and determination have shaped the life of Bob Lujano. To learn about his journey and to be in his presence is to more fully understand the true meaning of inspiration, hope, faith, and joy and above all, the love of life."

–Jennifer Chandler Stevenson, 1976 Olympic Gold Medalist, Diving

"It has been such a joy and privilege to read this book. I know that I am forever changed. The story was moving and hit deeply on many levels. I loved the different voices used and the way you brought your experience and perspectives to light. It was vulnerable and so helpful for me in seeing myself. Well done."

–Lena Giron

"Bob's story and indomitable spirit are absolutely what make him one of the most uniquely inspirational people I've ever met. I will never stop being grateful for his example and all he and Tara have taught me through this incredible story."

–Mick Silva, Editor, "For a higher purpose"

"Eckhart Tolle, the spiritual philosopher, wrote that there are two parts of life—your life and your life situation. Everyone's life situation is filled with the constant toils and struggles that we all encounter; your *life* is underneath your *life situation* and represents the spiritual-metaphysical interface that comes with being part of a collective group that includes all of humanity. Most people will read this book and see Bob's life situation, filled with the day-to-day challenges of performing everyday tasks. How does one with no arms or legs wake up, get dressed, and go to work? The word 'adaptation' was created for people like Bob who figure out ways to stay in the fold of humanity and the lexicon does not include, "I can't do that." But Bob's testimonial about his life journey, or life situation, is a tiny element of the more important aspect of this book, his life. Bob's professional and spiritual journey has taken him to places that most will never see. His amazing insight into the world of darkness and light, and its very contrast, will deeply move you. What most people will take away from the book is learning about Bob's life situation. But what you really need to take away from the book is the life underneath Bob's life situation, that we are all one body, one mind and one spirit and that Bob's contribution to the universe is an extremely valuable part of this richness."

–Dr. James Rimmer

"Bob teaches us all a critical life lesson that our true self and the source of human goodness lies in our mind, character, and spirit. His story also raises the importance of family in those good events, and the traumatic events, that shape our lives. Bob's refusal to let his physical state define him as a person is something we can and should all learn from."

–Jeff Underwood, President, Lakeshore Foundation

NO ARMS,
NO LEGS,
NO PROBLEM

WHEN LIFE HAPPENS,
YOU CAN WISH TO DIE OR CHOOSE TO LIVE

BOB LUJANO AND TARA SCHIRO

Write with Grace

Write with Grace

www.NoArmsNoLegsNoProblem.com
Tara@WriteWithGrace.com
BobL@Lakeshore.org

First Edition

Cover Design: Streetlight Graphics
Cover Photo by: Cary Norton www.CaryNorton.com
Bob's Author Photo by: Jill Anders
Tara's Author Photo by: Nicole Pollard Photography

ISBN paperback 978-0-9863053-0-6
ISBN hardcover 978-0-9863053-1-3
ISBN ebook 978-0-9863053-2-0

Disabled: "to make incapable or ineffective; especially to deprive of physical, moral, or intellectual strength."

—Websters.com

"Since I lost my limbs, society has tried to define me.

I've gone from crippled to handicapped, to physically challenged, and now to disabled.

As far as I'm concerned, I've always just been Bob."

Table of Contents

"Do not be anxious about anything, but in every situation, by prayer and petition, with thanksgiving, present your requests to God. And the peace of God, which transcends all understanding, will guard your hearts and your minds in Christ Jesus."

Philippians 4:6-7 NIV

Introduction

or

"How to Eat Pizza with Your Elbows"

MY HEART JUMPED THE DAY I first laid eyes on him. He was two feet tall and sitting in the middle of a queen-sized bed in a hotel room in Moraga, California. It was January, 2007.

His sister, Lisa, greeted me at the door and I tried to match her excitement but my mouth went dry as I forced a smile to hide my incredulity. This man had no arms or legs. And his name was Bob.

My family and I had come to see him speak at St. Mary's College as a way of formal introduction after being commissioned to write his book. Even though I had previously spoken to him on the phone to make arrangements, I was now completely off balance seeing him in person. He welcomed me with a kindness I did not understand. The warmth he radiated was palpable—and confusing.

With a beaming smile he scooted to the edge of the bed and extended his arm. "Hi, I'm Bob! How are you?"

Shocked, thank you very much.

I took his right limb, severed at the elbow and full of scars, into my right hand and shook as if nothing was amiss. His eyes carried an obvious peace and joy but I was blinded by my own inabilities. My eyes darted around the room looking for answers to the questions I was forming in my head, all having to do with *how*.

How does he get up and down from the high bed?

How does he reach to brush his teeth?

How does he shower? Shave? Go to the bathroom?

I did not see evidence of equipment or special aides to get him through the ordeal of tasks I always took for granted. I maintained my smile as we went through the perfunctory questions.

"How was your trip?"

"What time should we leave for your talk?"

I'm sure he knew I was uncomfortable and was scanning for evidence rather than being genuinely pleased to meet him. But he gave no sign of it.

About an hour later, Bob, Lisa, and I drove to the college and had dinner with the president, the student representatives, and the person in charge of scheduling Bob to speak.

Now in the role of observer, I could use them as a mirror to my own emotions. They scrambled a bit when we entered the room. Their faces betrayed their welcome with a look of what-were-we-thinking-when-we-planned-this-dinner? *Does he need anything different or special in order to feed himself?*

I could see they were second-guessing everything. Twelve of us sat around a banquet table to share a meal. Tension blanketed the room. Our hosts grappled to find equilibrium as they tried to make small talk but keep their composure and try not to stare. It was good they had food to put in their mouths to keep them from simply hanging open. Eating was a way to move forward and staring into your plate gives the mind time to regroup.

The questions asked as we ate had obviously been rehearsed. A couple of times the president or the club leader prompted the students. "Didn't you want to ask Bob about disabled services for students on campus?"

"Oh, yes," a student would respond. "Um…" and then the question would come. I could see the wheels turn in their head as they tried to remember themselves. I felt bad for them. They plainly wanted to ask different questions now that Bob was right in front of them. This encounter was no longer about the agenda that had prompted them to invite him to speak.

It was now personal.

Bob sat in between Lisa and me and I wasn't sure if I should help him or not. I waited to see if she would feed him, as did everyone else at the table. Nope. He picked up his fork with his elbows and dug right into his salad. I glanced at our hosts, then at Bob. He ate with assertion.

"This is great, thank you for this wonderful dinner. It was very nice of you to invite me," he said in between bites.

The whole group burst in at once, letting out some anxiety. "You're welcome!" "It's great to have you!" "Yes, what a great dinner." "We need to thank the culinary team."

Awkward.

Bob quietly asked Lisa to butter his bread and cut his chicken and then apologized to the table, saying something about cutting and buttering not being a part of his skill set as he picked up his glass in his elbows and took a drink. He graciously asked them questions about the college, repeated several times how grateful he was to be there, and seemed generally oblivious to the tension coming from those who didn't know what to do with themselves in his presence.

After dinner the group walked through the campus to the building where Bob would give his presentation. There was a long concrete incline between two of the buildings. It seemed steep to me; enough to make me lean forward a little as I walked. I became winded. My first inclination was to reach out to the handles on Bob's chair to give him a push up the hill. My hands went forward but could not find a place to grab; his chair does not have handles. My second inclination was to put my hands flat on the back of his chair, along his shoulders, and push that way. But this seemed too personal and embarrassing. I didn't want to be rude and not help him, but I didn't want to push on his shoulders either. I resolved to walk red faced up the hill and marvel at the fact that he could push up the hill unassisted and at the same time felt guilty for not helping.

His silent statement of independence made me uncomfortable. He had no idea I was behind him trying to decide how I could help him but it didn't matter. He didn't need help, which is why he rolls through life in a chair with no handles. He is able.

By the time my family and I heard him speak later that night to a crowd of 200 college students, I was thoroughly confused. He briefly mentioned his illness and the reason for his amputations but the majority of the presentation was about the importance of a healthy lifestyle through diet and exercise. No mention of childhood trauma, no visible anger or resentment, no mention of how he is mistreated as a disabled person, no real story. I didn't get it. I could feel the confusion from the audience around me.

We hung on his every word but it felt as if we were being robbed of the backstory, and any reason for his seemingly casual take on life. We needed him to start from the beginning and explain the journey, the choices that brought him physical and mental health. We knew from the flyer that advertised his presentation that he was successful and independent but how did he get there and why didn't he talk about it?

Over the next seven years my quest to answer "*who* is this man and *how* does he get through life" became something of an obsession. As his writer, I wanted to go back and fill in all the gaps, starting with the questions I had first formed in the hotel room. I wanted the whole story, but it soon became a challenge of *be careful what you ask for.*

As I dug deeper and moved from "how does he live" to "who is this man," problems surfaced; mainly, my own confusion. His account began to feel like a puzzle I needed to solve. There were outside influences, underlying themes—tragedy, disability, family, employment, the general public—that were bigger than Bob and sometimes not about him at all but so important to who he is. So many people play a part in his life and yet it's Bob's story.

Bob is just grateful; the first version he gave me read like a giant thank you card. And therein was the real problem: how can Bob speak to all of the things he is forced to deal with on a daily basis that aren't really about him? And how can I convince him to tell us the deeper story that gives context to the gratitude? Trying to decide how this story would be told seemed insurmountable for several years.

We finally decided to use three voices to give the totality of Bob's life: Bob's, mine, and the omniscient narrator.

1. Chapters 2-5 narrate the night Bob got sick up until the day

he awoke from his coma. We gathered the stories from Bob's father, sister, cousin, uncle, grandmother, and surgeon to tell that part of his life.

2. I continue my encounter with Bob in chapters 10 and 15 as honestly as I can. I did find anger and resentment, but not where I expected it. What I discovered along the way was truly a gift.

3. Bob's voice as he narrates his life is not dramatic, but matter-of-fact. He writes the way he lives: grateful, gracious and humble.

What I love about the simplicity of his words is that he's a guy who wants to live like everyone else. There are lessons in what he leaves out as well as in what he includes. He doesn't complain because to him, that's not living. The joy and peace I saw in his eyes that first day are not a put-on; they are a deep-seeded result of the choice to live.

I look back at that day at St. Mary's to remember how incapable I was of seeing a fellow human being for who he was. I did not handle that encounter with grace; that was the day I was smacked with my own disability.

For seven years I strained to understand Bob and his zeal for life. I found he is an inspiration, a man living life to the full, touching and changing the lives of everyone around him.

This is the story I've wanted to tell; how he moved past the days that look like nightmares, how he chose a life of substance and independence, and how he gives back to teach what he's learned. I hope you will see *who* Bob is, from the beginning, and why living with no arms and no legs is truly not a problem.

—Tara Schiro

"Oh yes, you shaped me first inside, then out; you formed me in my mother's womb. I thank you, High God—you're breathtaking! Body and soul, I am marvelously made! Like an open book, you watched me grow from conception to birth; all the stages of my life were spread out before you, the days of my life all prepared before I'd even lived one day."

Psalm 139:13-16 MSG

1

Shooter

I SAW THE UGLY SIDE OF life in the nine years before my illness. My mom walked out on us, my dad ruled with a leather belt, and we moved a lot from Kansas, to Texas, to Ohio, to Texas and then back to Kansas. I don't like to talk about it and I certainly don't choose to dwell on this time of my life. But positive or negative, it is my foundation and it shaped me into who I am today.

Hardship was a factor in how I handled my illness and recovery. Discipline was the order of the day back then and even though it was dysfunctional and abusive, I would need every ounce of the mental toughness it gave me to get through the hell that was coming.

When the game changed and became do-or-die, I would be stuck with the life I had been given thus far. There is no way to prepare for a disease that necessitates the removal of all four limbs, especially at age nine. It comes and you take it. And all your previous life experiences come into play to define how you handle it. Your foundation either raises you up strong or crushes you in the rubble with one final blow.

I would soon find out which story it would be for me.

In many regards, my upbringing was not very different from many Midwestern boys in the mid-seventies. We all wanted to play baseball. We all wanted to be George Brett, Nolan Ryan or my favorite, Pete Rose.

I can still remember the day my father took me to Riverfront Stadium in 1974 to see the Reds play. I can't remember who they

1

played or even if they won, I just know Pete Rose was playing and I was there to watch him.

Pete was stocky and stout. He gave 110% on the field playing with reckless abandon. He was an all-out hustler and was given the nickname Charlie Hustle. He could play multiple positions—third base, outfield, first base, shortstop—he did everything. He used everything he had to the best of his ability. He became the all-time leading hitter.

When I started playing, I gave baseball my all to do it just like Pete. I was given the nickname Shooter because I could shoot the ball right where I wanted it. I started off with tee ball and my competitive nature showed up. I had natural abilities and was nominated to be team leader.

My obsession continued as I watched the Reds play on television. I stayed outside for hours and threw the ball against the wall to practice catching. I played nine-inning games in my head, pitching, hitting, throwing and making every play myself. I even worked on sliding head first into a base to do it just like the pros. The Reds were the best team, Pete Rose was the best player, and I was going to be the next Pete Rose and that was it.

My efforts were paying off. When we moved again, I was a member of the Ferris Falcons in Irving, Texas. I remember my Dad telling me, "You've got to give everything you can to stop the ball." He taught me the fundamentals of positioning your glove, your feet, and your body before the ball is even hit. He showed me pictures and said, "This is how Pete Rose does it." I was determined to be the best shortstop in the history of tee ball.

There were many occasions while playing for the Falcons that I came home with seam imprints of the baseball on my forehead. Although it hurt, I thought I looked cool because I was hustling like Pete, just like my father had instructed.

That 1975 team went on to win the city of Irving Tee Ball Championship. I remember when my trophy arrived; it was the first trophy of any sports accomplishment. Unfortunately, I was so proud of the trophy that I had to show it to everyone I came in contact with

2

and eventually it broke. I don't think it lasted two weeks. It didn't matter because we were still the city champs of 1975.

I knew no other way to gain my dad's approval than through sports. I always wanted to please him so when he happened to be at a game, it would inevitably turn out to be a bad game because I was trying too hard.

I tried so hard to make an impression. One time I struck out and he was visibly upset. I threw the bat from the embarrassment of messing up. He didn't see many of my games because he was on the road much of the time with his job and came home late when he was in town. So playing to perfection was an added pressure when he was around.

As I added other sports, it did finally occur to me that pleasing my dad was a high priority. Not just because he was Dad, but because this seemed to be the only thing that really bonded us. Sports, in general, were instrumental in us even having a relationship.

Along with abuse, playing a sport was the other family legacy passed down through the generations. My dad, proud of his success as the first Hispanic quarterback in his all-white high school, had to prove himself over and over again.

My Grandpa Bill played and coached baseball before forming the first Mexican fast-pitch tournament in 1938 in Newton, KS. It still goes on today every Fourth of July. One of my cousins, Paul Garibay, was drafted by the Phillies.

I'm glad my dad had a glove on my hand at an early age because I truly feared the man, so desperately wanted to do something to make him proud of me. I always felt before my illness that I was not really loved by him. Not that he didn't love me, I know he did, it's just that between all the yelling and whipping, it left me wondering if there was anything good I could do to make my dad happy. Sports seemed to be the thing I could use to make him forget whatever I'd done to make him angry.

My father disciplined my sister and I severely and thoroughly so we would learn from our mistakes. He was the guy in charge and we were to do what he said or we paid the consequences. Usually discipline is passed on. Grandpa Bill was a disciplinarian. Dad says he always knew where he stood with him. He says my Grandpa Bill used to use his fist. My dad never used his fist with us, but he did use the belt.

The worst whipping I ever got was when I was four years old. My mom, dad, Lisa and I were in the family car on the way home from church. I was dressed in a suit. I had to go to the bathroom so I asked my dad to pull over. My dad wouldn't. I couldn't hold it any longer so I urinated in my suit. I knew I would get whipped. I wanted to clean up so I darted for the bathroom as soon as we stepped inside the house.

When I got out of the shower my dad called me into his room and before I could get dressed, he whipped me. A leather belt on wet, bare skin is very painful. The message was supposed to be "don't urinate in car," but the message I learned instead was to fear my father. Fear of disappointing him, of not living up to his expectations, it hounded me. If I didn't do what he said, I would soon feel the sting of the belt. To this day, I don't like to disappoint people.

There were days as we grew older that we got whipped and didn't know why, wasn't told why, just got pulled in and whipped. On one particular occasion, we were playing in the living room with our cousins. We were told several times to settle down. My cousin flipped me in the air and I fell on my shoulder. We all got whipped for not listening. Then we went to the hospital to take care of my broken collarbone. When we arrived home we got whipped again for not listening!

Strangely, though she left when I was five, I always felt closer to my mom. I saw her as soft-spoken and laid-back, not one to put her foot down and I felt bonded to her in this way because I saw myself as a more laid-back person not putting my foot down.

When she finally left, she had walked out several times and each time my dad talked her into coming back. I've tried to remember her comings and goings, what she wore, what she said, but I can't. My sister Lisa was seven and she remembers more than I do, but self-preservation is strong with her as well. It's amazing how the mind can tune out certain things, possibly to protect us from pain.

We don't even have any pictures of her. Lisa had a habit of standing at the bathroom counter to watch as she put on makeup and fixed her hair. It was the 70's and she had a long, layered hairstyle. She typically wore bell-bottom blue jeans and t-shirts.

She wasn't fancy but she was pretty, about 5'7" with a slender build, green eyes and a light Hispanic complexion. As Lisa watched, she would say things in front of the large mirror.

"I never wanted you kids. Your dad did."

She used to tell my dad to "take those kids and shove them."

She didn't like to stay at home "waiting for those kids" to come back from school. She wanted more out of life. So she got herself a boyfriend who promised to show her the world. She began to leave us by ourselves in the apartment for longer periods when Dad was away at work or out of town on business.

And then one day, bowling bag in hand, she announced she was leaving. As Lisa and I sat and watched from the kitchen table in our tiny apartment in Dallas, I had no idea what was happening.

We had already learned at five and seven the cruelty of her words and the continuous threats to leave us for good. But we still couldn't imagine that she would really do it. The bowling bag however, was a tip off that something was up. She had her clothes packed in there. It was the middle of the afternoon and she said she was going bowling and she walked out the door.

After several hours, we began to get hungry and looked for something to eat. The reality was sinking in that she'd meant it this time—she wasn't coming back.

Lisa climbed up on the kitchen counter to reach the yellow phone on the wall. She held the heavy receiver with the long squiggly cord in one hand and with her other hand, put her small fingers into the big circular holes, rotating them around and around. I recall the slow buzz the phone made as the dial returned to its original position.

She was trying to call my dad at work but she didn't know the number. She kept calling the wrong people.

An operator came on the line and Lisa asked her for Dad's office number. The operator said she didn't know, even though Lisa gave her the name of the company. She said she couldn't help. She thought Lisa was just messing around with the phone.

We didn't have 911 back then, so Lisa kept asking the operator for help but the woman kept telling her to hang up. The operator called back to tell my parents she was playing with the phone but Lisa kept answering. When she demanded to speak to our mother or father, Lisa told her they weren't home. The operator scolded her for playing around and hung up. We climbed down from the counter and waited.

It began to get dark.

Later that night, my dad came home. He piled us into the car to search for our mother. We went to apartment complexes, drove around town, and eventually showed up outside a bar/nightclub that my dad thought she might be hanging out in. She wasn't there which was a good thing because he was quite upset. I believe he would have kicked any rear-end he found, including his wife's.

We waited in the car late into the night. Lisa and I peeked out the window and hid in the backseat so no one would see us. We were scared and knew this was not what a normal family would be doing with their evening time.

It was a long time before she eventually returned home, but she only stayed for a very brief visit. She didn't want to be married. And she definitely didn't want kids.

My dad said, "If you leave again, don't bother coming back. Leave the kids alone. The door is closed."

Even tough men can only take so much.

The next time I would see her was four years later at my hospital bedside where she sat crocheting.

Did she speak to me? Did she hug me and tell me it was all going to be okay? Did she say that she was sorry, or that she loved me? I can't remember. She only stayed for a few hours.

At the age of eighteen I was having nightmares about her safety so Lisa and I tracked her down and met her for coffee. She barely talked. She offered no apologies and seemed miserable. Her boyfriend had not shown her the world, but the sting of rejection. That was the last time we saw her. I don't know where she is or even if she is alive.

I suppose it's obvious there was a void in my life when she was gone for good. Her absence left a strange dynamic in our home. It's unnatural for a mom to abandon her kids. I've asked myself many times, Did she leave because of me? Was it something I did? Were

Lisa and I not good enough? She said many times to our face that she didn't want us.

But here's the rub: though verbally she rejected me, and then physically abandoned me, emotionally she was my protection from my father. I was attached to her in the way most five-year-olds are. When my father disciplined me, I was afraid. I ran to her and hid, and my mother comforted me there and I felt safer.

It was a shock to think she could leave us. I was terrified. I couldn't imagine what could make her want to walk out on us. My parents were in their early twenties when we were born, a difficult age for anyone to be a parent. My Grandma Hope says she hated to come visit us because we were "always in trouble for something" and getting whipped. Running to Mom, becoming attached to her, even identifying with her as my same temperament, when she left with her bowling bag, my protection was gone.

I suddenly knew I was on my own and took extra precaution. I dreaded getting in trouble. I'd wanted my father's approval before, now I needed it like air.

I would look out the window wishing my mom would come home. But when I was on the baseball field pretending to be Pete, I was happy. I played hard to connect with dad. I didn't know any other way.

He promised to take care of us and he did. He told us not to worry; we were going to be okay. He tried hard after that to be both mom and dad. Dinner was always on the table and our clothes were clean. He did the best he could and Lisa and I are so appreciative of his efforts.

I'm also grateful for how he handled our mom's departure. He controlled his anger in front of us which made the transition a little easier. He never cursed her. In fact, he never mentioned her name again. She was gone and that was that. No use crying over spilled milk, just move on. He was strong for us. I know he was hurt deeply when she left but he was careful to keep his emotions in check when we were around. His main concern now was his children, not himself. I have a ton of respect for how he controlled his anger in this terrible time. His display of good character was a great life lesson.

There came a time though, not too long after she left, when he realized he just couldn't take care of us on his own. He couldn't have two young children at home alone while he worked. We piled into the family car and drove from Dallas, Texas, all the way to Newton, Kansas. Our suitcases of clothes were in the trunk. Being the trusting and believing children that we were, we never thought twice of what our dad was doing.

As we pulled into the driveway of the little avocado green house that would be our new home, I quickly caught site of the empty field across the street and the Catholic Church beside it. Instinctively my nerves began to calm. We didn't know our Grandma Hope very well but this would soon change. My grandparents and my Aunt Mary greeted us warmly at the door but the mood was somber.

After the pleasantries about the trip, we sat in the family room and listened to my dad as he humbly told them my mother had left. Reconciliation had been attempted several times but it didn't work. She was gone for good.

"I need help with my children," he said. "I don't know what I'm going to do but I know that I need them to be taken care of while I get us back on our feet."

Lisa and I sat wide-eyed on the floor and looked up at the adults on the couch. My grandmother was heartbroken and cried to herself. My aunt let big tears roll down her cheeks. My grandfather didn't say much of anything and my Uncle Richard said a few swear words against my mother, to which my grandmother said "shush" and "not in front of the kids."

They all said they would help with whatever needed to be done.

After a meal and the details finalized, my dad drove away and left us there. In hindsight, I don't begrudge him the decision. But at the time, it wasn't easy. I was only five. First my mom and then my dad; they both abandoned us.

One of the first lessons I remember Grandma Hope teaching me was to always love and appreciate my sister Lisa. Despite not having both of our parents, we would always have each other. I'm grateful for this lesson, grateful that Grandma had the foresight to pass along the wisdom she learned early in life: the hard reality is that when families break apart or tragedy strikes, you have to cling to whatever is left and make it stronger. No sense in worrying about what you don't have, take care of what you *do* have and build from there.

She was right. Lisa was all I had left. It was us against the world. The relationship I have with Lisa has been my rock to this day, even though we now live thousands of miles apart.

Most of the responsibility to take care of us was placed on my grandmother but she lovingly treated us like her own. She once told Lisa that God had sent her to us because she needed us as much as we needed her. She said she was dying inside of loneliness. We were not a burden to her.

My grandfather was a different story. Lisa used to cry herself to sleep at night because she could hear grandfather harassing grandmother at bedtime, asking, "When is Bob going to get these kids?" He resented our presence. My father couldn't take us home but he never wavered in his love for us. During the first year he drove every Friday to Kansas, 365 miles, arriving at 1:00 a.m. to spend the weekend with us. During the next three years he cut it back to every other weekend.

We had a new family. At first, life at Grandma Hope's was as normal and pleasant as could be expected. My grandmother's house was disciplined but we were well taken care of. There was always enough food and always someone around. We were never alone.

My grandparents were also helping Aunt Mary with her three boys after her divorce. They lived in a house nearby but spent many overnights through the weekends with us. Life with my cousins helped soothe the early wounds of rejection and abandonment, and the five of us, me, Lisa, Paul, Willie, and Johnny, spent a great deal of time together.

I played baseball in the empty lot with my cousin, Paul. In the long days of summer, from sunup to sundown we played catch in the field, threw the ball around, and played on the same teams. We dreamed of being professional ball players. We wanted to be the best athletes we could be. Between us kids, we were one big happy family. We were more than cousins; we were brothers in arms amid the backdrop of so much pain and dysfunction that was about to intensify. Lisa and I could count on each other and the cousins were an extension of that.

9

The greatest blessing Grandma Hope bestowed on me was teaching me the importance of having a relationship with God. She impressed upon me that being part of the Catholic Church wasn't just about sitting in the pew. It was about being involved as a server, having a prayer life, having a spiritual life, and going through catechism.

Our Lady of Guadalupe Church in Newton, Kansas was literally 100 paces from my grandmother's front door and we attended every Sunday during those four years. I started as an altar boy at the age of seven and continued until my illness. Every Sunday morning, I loved getting up and going to church. I could not wait to get there. My role and purpose for getting up on Sunday was to serve in the program of the mass. I loved it! What an honor it was, especially considering that Our Lady of Guadalupe Church had been founded and built by my Grandpa Bill.

I still remember the first time I got to ring the chime during the blessing of the Eucharist. It was important to get the timing down. I had practiced all week for this moment. I choked. I rang it late. This is the most important blessing of the whole mass, the most important moment of the whole Catholic Church! Father Riley glanced over at me waiting for me to ring the chime. He sort of looked at me like, "You want me to come over there and do it?" That was it. From then on I rang the chime with perfect timing.

I was drawn to more than just attending and serving. Tiny seeds were being planted in my young soul for a deep relationship with Jesus. I didn't fully understand this until much later, but the attraction I felt was real; like a magnetic force of safety and security pulling me in. There was peace there. I had a purpose. I felt the love of my grandma and the adrenaline of the ball field inside that sanctuary. It all made sense in the presence of God. The relationship that was planted was about more than just going to church; it was about the joy of living.

Grandma Hope was the first person to show me unconditional love. Her warm and generous spirit filled the gaping hole left by my mother. But my world turned upside down again when one day it became crystal clear why my grandmother had told Lisa she was dying of loneliness and that God had sent us to her because she needed us as much as we needed her.

I was eight years old now and it was spring of '78 and my grandparents were arguing in the kitchen. It escalated. My grandpa Bill grabbed Grandma Hope and threw her up against the fridge, balled up his fist, and started punching her like he was in a barroom fight with a man. Lisa started crying and I took her into the living room and we waited there, but I couldn't stand it. I had to run back to the kitchen.

I yelled at my grandfather to stop but he wouldn't listen. He shoved her into the dishwasher and then to the stairs. She tried to fight back and kept screaming for him to stop but she was no match against his rage. The beating lasted five or ten minutes. There was blood everywhere. My grandmother finally staggered to the dining room and sat down and I buried my head in her lap and cried uncontrollably. Still to this day it remains the worst thing I ever saw in my life. It's always in the back of my mind.

The police came that day but they left without making any arrest or charge. Grandma Hope was bruised all over her face and body. She was in such pain that she couldn't be hugged or touched for a few weeks. She took it easy but carried on with her daily life, taking care of us kids the best she could. Her bruises lasted a month.

Lisa and I stayed away from Grandpa Bill for several weeks. We were as careful as possible, in terror of igniting his anger, but since we were all in the same house, it made for awkward living. One day he had had enough of me and Lisa ignoring him. The four of us were in the kitchen together before church and I reached up to the cabinet to get my vitamins at the same time he reached for a glass. Our arms touched and I flinched and this triggered his rage. He punched me with the back of his fist square on my nose.

"Aren't you going to say good morning to me?" he yelled.

My nose started bleeding uncontrollably and I started to freak out. Then he went to Lisa who was wide-eyed and stiff with fear.

"Aren't you going to say good morning to me, either?" and he punched her in the jaw.

Now Lisa was screaming and crying. Luckily, Uncle Richard was in the basement and hearing the ruckus, he came up and yelled at his dad to leave the kitchen. He took us to the emergency room because my nose would not stop bleeding.

The police came again and this time Grandpa Bill was arrested. He spent the night in jail but was back the next morning. I knew from then on, he was a man not to be messed with. When I helped him in the garden, I always did what I was told and learned not to be late because it upset him. The fear of my father became the fear of my grandfather. I learned early on to be perfect and not get in trouble.

What possesses a man to be so violent; the anger over the violence done to him? I didn't know this then and I lost a lot of respect for him when I saw him punch Grandma and Lisa. After that day, Uncle Richard told us that Grandpa Bill had been abusing his wife for thirty-five years. She had said that she couldn't leave him because she had nowhere to go and had young children to raise. In the three years we were there, there were other altercations but we didn't know about them. Maybe I was too young to understand, or maybe I didn't want to know. Uncle Richard didn't say whether or not he himself had ever been on the receiving end, but I know my dad was many times.

Uncle Richard told us that Grandpa Bill did not have a father. He was adopted and abused. But he'd won a purple heart in the WWII Pacific Island Battles.

My Grandma Hope was born a twin (her sister later died in infancy) and orphaned at a young age. She had to endure many foster homes that were cruel and insincere; she said she was only given to them to be used for labor. Once the tasks were over, she was orphaned again, only to be used in the same manner by other foster parents. She survived and forged an unbreakable bond with her siblings. They were placed into different foster homes but despite the separation and distance, her brother and sisters kept in contact.

To create the life of love she always wanted, she married my Grandpa Bill and filled her home with six children of her own. One of them died in childbirth. But because she had only known abuse her entire life, she didn't see until it was too late that the man she married to be her savior turned out to be her next abuser. I figured that if my grandma could endure the life she was given and then thirty-five years of abuse by her husband, then I could endure one beating from him.

I did my chores as I was told and then made a bee-line to the baseball field with my cousins. There was no fear there. We could be rough-and-tumble and play hard and be ourselves without worry.

The last season before my illness, the last time I played for Our Lady of Guadalupe in the summer of 1978, we were undefeated. It was the final game of the playoffs to decide the league champion. We had home court advantage. The entire family was there, including my dad. Everybody's family was there. This was a big deal.

The other team was last up to bat and the bases were loaded. We had to stop them. The chatter from the field intensified and the crowd responded with their own shouts of encouragement. We could let one run in and still win the game, but no more. We needed to concentrate and get the next batter out. To our delight, the next batter was a girl!

"Piece of cake!" came the shouts from both the outfield and the infield.

"Easy out!" I taunted from shortstop.

She ignored us and walked straight to home base, bat held high in position. The pitch was in. *Crack!* We watched the ball fly over our heads as it kept going and going over the fence. A grand slam. The players on all three bases jumped for joy as they paraded in and pile-dived on top of one another. The girl ran proudly around the bases and jumped into the team piled at home plate. We lost the championship. To a girl! That hurt. We were undefeated until she came along.

In fact, it still hurts to think about it.

"Why, you do not even know what will happen tomorrow. What is your life? You are a mist that appears for a little while and then vanishes."

James 4:14 NIV

2

Now I Lay Me Down to Sleep

I T WAS JANUARY 6, 1979, in Newton, Kansas, population 16,000. A few hundred kids were packed into the Starlite Skating Rink, a red building on 3rd Street. The cousins had been there many times. Nothing was ever remarkable to report after a night of whirling around to the loud music, except the rare occasion they could afford a pop to quench their thirst or the boy who broke his arm after a race gone badly.

This Saturday night seemed like all the others. But it wasn't. Something was lurking in the air and waiting for Bobby as he followed his cousins inside to rent skates. He didn't know he was skating his last skate. What he did know was how to go fast, and he used that to his advantage.

"Tag! You're it, Lisa!" Bobby blew past his sister with lightning speed before slowing down behind the man with the big hair and the whistle. He looked back to see how close his cousins were to catching him and then dodged in-and-out of traffic to widen the gap. Streams of disco light bounced across the floor to the beat of "Le Freak," by Chic.

Nothing out of the ordinary. Nothing but the familiar feeling of the wheels spinning under his feet.

As he danced along, his sister and cousins came up beside him. Lisa and Johnny, 11, Paul, 7, and Willie, 5.

"We're thirsty. Let's get a drink."

15

They crowded into the line at the water fountain. Each took a turn, winding the handle and waiting for the spray of water from the bottom like a miniature geyser. They all talked at once, bumping and pushing.

"I won," said Paul.

"Liar! I had the most points!" argued Johnny.

Bobby laughed, took a drink, and wiped his mouth, pointing toward the rink at the couples holding hands as they skated.

"Couple's skate!" Bobby said.

"Why don't you go hold that girl's hand?" teased Paul, motioning to a dark-haired girl with long braids. "I think she likes you!"

"Shut up, Paulie," Bobby said, sneaking a glance.

"Yeah, shut up Paul!" said Lisa.

"Ooh, someone's in love," said Johnny.

"Am not," Bobby said. "I don't even know her!"

Johnny and Willie started a sing-song, "Bobby and her, sitting in the tree. K-I-S-S-I-N-G! First comes love, then comes marriage, then comes baby in the baby carriage!"

"I said shut up!" and Bobby shoved Johnny and they tussled until the guy with the big hair and whistle broke them up. The cousins filed out onto the rink, laughing and pushing.

The music changed and they put their arms into the air as they skated out.

"Y.M.C.A.! Y.M.C.A!"

Bobby tried to keep up with the movements, laughing at Paul when he fell, and skating fast past him. Lisa laughed performing the motions perfectly through the blur of bodies and Bobby went faster and faster.

So free. So safe.

The whirl of the disco lights, the blare of the music, it was intoxicating. The girl with the braids smiled as she passed and then turned to face him as she skated backwards, her arms in a Y.

"Hi!" she said.

"Hi!" Bobby said, a huge smile on his face.

Not to be outdone, he moved beside her to skate backwards but

16

he swayed and was thrown off balance. It made her laugh and though Bobby didn't fall, it wasn't pretty.

The D.J. called over the loud speaker, "All boys! All boys!"

The man with the big hair blew his whistle and the girls left the rink. The boys sped up as "Wipeout" blared over the speakers.

"I'm gonna take you!" said Johnny as he blew by.

"No, you're not!" Bobby shouted back.

The older boys seemed to go a hundred miles an hour around the rink and the cousins tried to keep up with them. Around and around in an aggressive competition.

Then, the girls. "MacArthur Park" by Donna Summer, and the girls skated in leisurely groups of three or four, carrying on conversations. Bobby tried to watch the girl with the braids.

Finally, the familiar "Last Dance" started and the boys clamored back onto the rink.

Bobby didn't want it to end.

Lisa, Paul, Willie, Johnny, and Bobby skated as a group, as many laps as possible before the music was gone.

The lights came up. The DJ called for all skaters to clear the rink. And Bobby sped around the giant circle one last time before the man with the whistle gave him the warning. Reluctantly, but happily, Bobby skated off.

They found their shoes and dropped their skates in the big pile by the rental desk. They put on their heavy coats and gloves to wait outside for Uncle Richard.

Bobby had just cashed-in his last ticket. He was now on a collision course with destiny. The biting chill on their cheeks provided soothing relief from the hot rink and cooled their sweaty bodies.

As they piled into the car, they recounted the night's games and activities, and Bobby giggled at the stories as his cousins all talked at once, unaware everything had already changed forever.

As they burst into the house, Willie called, "Grams, we're starving! Is there anything to eat?"

"You kids need to get to bed. I want you fresh for mass in the morning," she said.

Lisa obeyed and went to her bedroom on the main floor. As the only girl, she got the whole thing to herself. Grandma and Grandpa slept in the room next to her. The boy cousins headed down to the basement where Johnny slept on the couch and Paul, Willie and Bobby shared a queen-size bed in the tiny orange room. They flicked on the light-switch covered by the glow-in-the dark cereal box sticker.

Dark brown paneling covered the far wall and orange curtains hung in the tiny window looking out on a staircase.

"My legs are so tired," Bobby said.

"You were going so fast!" said Paul.

Uncle Richard followed them down the stairs.

"You boys keep quiet and get to sleep." He went inside the room next to theirs, closing the door behind him.

Willie made a face and pointed his finger at them, imitating Uncle Richard. They tried not to giggle as they put on their pajamas and crawled into bed.

The last thought in Bobby's head was to say his nightly prayers.

"Now I lay me down to sleep,
I pray the Lord my soul to keep.
If I should die before I wake,
I pray the Lord my soul to take."

He was suddenly so tired....

"Be strong and courageous. Do not be afraid or terrified because, for the Lord your God goes with you; he will never leave you nor forsake you."

Deuteronomy 31:6 NIV

3

Death in an Ambulance

SEVEN-YEAR-OLD PAUL STIRRED IN THE bed. He felt Willie's legs on top of him, sleeping sideways again. There was a noise coming from the other side of the bed but he was dreaming and couldn't rouse himself. His head was thick with sleep and confusion. The inaudible noise, more like a moan, came again from somewhere close by. Paul stirred again. Frustration and impatient breathing made him sit upright. He rubbed his eyes thinking this was still part of the dream.

"Paulie?" It was Bobby calling him.

"What's the matter?" asked Paul.

Bobby was agitated and sweating. "I feel like I'm on fire. I'm burning up."

"What do you want me to do?" asked Paul.

"Get me a cold rag," said Bobby.

It was midnight. Paul went into the bathroom and soaked a washcloth in the freezing water. He brought it back to Bob and placed it on his forehead.

"That feels good."

Paul got in on his side of the bed, pushed Willie's legs back to the middle and lay on his pillow.

"I'm so hot." Bobby couldn't get comfortable. "My back hurts."

Paul sighed. "I'll get you some Tylenol." He went back to the bathroom and returned with a glass of water and Tylenol. He flipped

21

the light on and stared at his cousin. He could tell something wasn't right. Bobby was sweating and his face was scrunched up like he was really uncomfortable. Paul didn't know what to do. He stood there for a moment, staring at Bob and then sat on the bed. Bobby pushed the covers off.

"Here," Paul said, holding out the water and Tylenol. "Take it."

"I need another rag," Bobby said.

This time, Paul moved a little quicker. When he came back, Bobby had taken off his shirt.

"I'm on fire," Bob said.

Paul wiped Bob's face with the cold cloth and then laid it on top of his head.

"Willie, get up," Paul said. "Go sleep on the couch." He grabbed Willie's arm and pulled him off the bed, guiding Willie to the end of the couch in the main room. A groan came from Bobby and Paul ran back.

"It hurts," Bobby was writhing. "I'm so hot." He took off his pajama pants and Paul went back and forth several times to dampen the cold rag.

It was now 2:00 a.m. and Paul was scared. He stood there all alone, his heart racing. He needed help. He looked at Uncle Richard's door, closed and locked, and decided to go get Lisa.

"Something's wrong with Bobby. We need to wake Grams."

"What's wrong with him?"

"He has a fever."

"I don't think you should wake her up."

"He's really sick, Lisa."

Lisa got out of bed and the two padded over to the open door of their grandparents' room. They paused, exchanged a hesitant look, and then went to Grandma Hope's side of the bed.

"Grams, Shooter's really sick. We need you to come downstairs," said Paul, shaking her shoulder.

"What's wrong with him?"

"I think he has a fever," said Paul.

"Oh, you kids. It's probably just a cold. Go back to bed." She rolled over and pulled the covers over her shoulders.

Lisa pulled Paul out of the room. "I told you," she whispered.

"Lisa, come with me. Please," begged Paul.

They made their way down the steps to the basement. Bobby was asleep. Lisa felt his forehead.

"He's pretty warm. Maybe we should give him a Tylenol."

"I already did."

"I'm going back to bed," said Lisa and she tiptoed back up the stairs.

Paul went and got another cold rag for Bobby's head. Somehow he knew this was more serious than the flu, but if Grams didn't think it was a big deal then maybe it wasn't. She was the adult. He was only seven. What did he know?

Still, his stomach turned with a terrifying helplessness and doom. He would do what he could for now to make Bobby comfortable, but he gave in to the fact there was nothing more he could do but wait until morning.

"Paulie." Bobby said. "Cold rag."

Paul went upstairs to get some ice to put in a towel. Clearly the water wasn't cold enough. When he came back down, Shooter was pulling at the sheets.

"It's so hot. Take them off," he groaned and writhed in pain.

Paul pulled the sheets and blankets onto the floor and handed the ice wrap to Bobby. By now, Paul was beside himself. He had never seen his cousin so agitated. This was bad, really bad. Alone and exhausted, he flipped off the light, went out to the other couch and sat down. He didn't know what else to do. He finally put his head on the armrest and closed his eyes.

LISA AWOKE FIRST ON THAT dark January morning. The house was eerily quiet; strange for a Sunday morning. Strange for a family who regularly attends early morning mass. She listened for her grandparents' footsteps. Silence. She tiptoed out of bed, past her grandparents' room, through the living room and through the door to the basement. She slowly descended the steep stairs in the dark. No noise down there, either. She thought it was unusual that her brother was still in bed, even though he had been sick in the night. He took seriously his duties as altar boy, always arriving on time. As she went through the main play area, Paul and Willie slept soundly on the couch, like bookends. Johnny was asleep on the other couch. Lisa walked toward Shooter's room. She put her hand on the light-switch and flipped it on with a heavy click. She blinked several times to adjust to the harshness of the bright light. Her brother lay horizontal and naked across the bed. The sheets, his pajamas, and underwear were all lying in a heap on the floor.

"What are you doing?" she shrieked and picked up his underwear and threw them across his privates. But Bobby lay motionless.

"Bobby?"

She stared at him for a moment waiting for movement. She poked his arm.

"Bobby?"

He mumbled something but Lisa couldn't hear. She put her face next to his.

"What's wrong?"

"Hot. So hot," he slurred. She put her hand against his scalding cheek. The mattress was soaked with sweat. Purple spots blotched his body. Lisa noticed the damp washcloth next to him.

"I'm going to wake up Gram. I'll be right back." She stopped at the couch to wake up her cousin. "Paul, wake up. He's got spots all over," and then she ran up the stairs to her grandmother's room. Her heart raced as she ran through the house.

It was morning. Grams would come this time. Paul came up behind her.

"Grams, you gotta wake up," she said. "Shooter's really sick. He has purple spots all over him."

"It's probably just the chicken pox," she moaned. "You kids need to calm down and get washed up for church."

But she got up and followed the kids downstairs, turning on the lights as they went. Grams fussed all the way down the basement.

"Oh, you kids...I don't know what to think..."

They were well-behaved children, but she was older and she let them know it. When they entered the tiny bedroom, the seriousness of the situation hit her with a thud. She looked at little Bobby strewn across the bed and realized this was more than a common childhood illness. The purple blotches were too big to be chicken pox. Waves of guilt began to wash over her, but it would not be until later when she heard the diagnosis that she would begin begging God to forgive her for not getting up in the night.

She'd been extra tired. She had worked hard and needed the rest. She made the sign of the cross across her chest.

"Oh, my God! Why didn't you wake me earlier? Go and get your Uncle Richard!" She again made the sign of the cross and began fussing about the sheets being all over the floor.

Lisa and Paul exchanged a glance and hot emotion reddened their faces. Paul wanted to cry. He had tried. Now he felt betrayed. The terror and loneliness he felt in the middle of the night came rushing back.

"I was up all night with him! He kept calling for a cold washcloth! He said the sheets were too hot so I put them on the floor!" He'd still done wrong and he blinked hard to stop the tears. Paul had no way of knowing that Grams was blaming herself, not him, but in her own fear and shame she couldn't bring herself to acknowledge it out loud.

"Don't just stand there, go wake your Uncle Richard!"

Paul burst into tears and rushed to Uncle Richard's door and began pounding. When the door opened, Grams took over.

"Richard, I need you to take Bobby to the emergency room. He's got the fever. I've got to get dressed!" And she went upstairs.

Richard was confused but dressed quickly. Johnny and Willie, awake from the commotion, stood silently in the doorway and stared at their cousin. Paul and Lisa examined Shooter's body while they grabbed his clothes to dress him. There were purple blotches and pin dots on his stomach, face, legs, feet, hands; they were everywhere. Lisa touched his feet, his legs. They were so hot. She tried to get Bobby dressed but he was so weak he was like a rag doll. Paul was so tired. He did his best to stop crying while he helped get Bobby dressed.

"No! Too hot!" Bobby screamed. "Leave me alone!" He fought and moaned from the pain shooting through his back.

"Maybe measles," said Grams, coming back in and trying to ease the fear in Paul and Lisa, the guilt welling up in her.

Lisa traced the dots on Bobby's feet and covered them with socks and shoes.

It would be the last time she saw him with legs. The last one to touch his feet.

They bundled him in his big red coat and Uncle Richard led him into the car.

The five of them watched as Bobby's hot breath hit the freezing air in short, labored puffs.

He would never walk on his own two feet again.

Flurries swirled around the car as they backed out of the driveway and drove away.

BOBBY WAS THE CLOSEST THING to a son to Uncle Richard. He had never married and had no children of his own but he treated all five of his niece and nephews as if they were his. He lived with his parents to help take care of the kids while his brother Bob Sr. and his sister Mary recovered from their respective divorces. Richard didn't complain; that's what family was for. Bob Sr. came from Texas every other weekend to visit his son and Lisa; but not this weekend.

It was up to Richard to take care of his nephew. Bobby moaned in the backseat.

"We're almost there, Shooter." The short drive to Bethel Deaconess Hospital in the frigid weather went surprisingly fast despite his nerves. He didn't like the way his nephew looked. He prayed it was only the measles, or the chicken pox, and convinced himself Bobby would be fine. They could be home for a late lunch. Uncle Richard parked the car and carried him into the ER, his shoes crunching the salt in the parking lot.

It was Sunday and Newton was a small town. The doctor needed to be called. The nurses undressed Bobby and put him into a hospital gown. The blotches on his arms and legs had gotten bigger, or maybe the cold air had just woken Richard up a little and he could see them better.

The nurses gave Bobby some medicine for the fever. Richard began to pace; it was taking much too long for the doctor to arrive. His nephew was obviously very sick and needed immediate attention.

"Where's the doctor?" he asked the nurses at the main station.

"She's on her way, sir."

"He should be here by now, shouldn't he?" He didn't like their casual attitude. His nephew was sick. They should be doing more than sitting there with their Cokes.

"Good morning, ladies. What do we have?"

Uncle Richard spun around to see a woman standing in a white coat with a stethoscope around her neck.

"Room five. Here's his chart."

"My nephew is really sick," began Richard too loudly. "He's got a high fever and purple splotches all over his body. He's in a lot of pain. What do you think it is?"

The doctor held up her hands. "Well, we're going to need to run some tests. Maybe it's measles or the flu. Let's take a look," she said.

Uncle Richard followed the doctor to Bobby's bedside and watched impatiently as she tested his pupils, felt his pulse, and made notes on the chart.

"Hmm, looks like he's going to be here for a while," she said.

"Why? What's wrong with him?" yelled Uncle Richard.

"I don't know, but I'm going to run some tests to see what we can find." She was so calm, which irritated him so much he had to leave the room.

He went out into the hall to the payphone and called home to report. They did not know what was wrong with him. He'd be staying a while. He'd let them know when they knew more.

Several hours later, there were still no answers. Bobby was in a private room and the doctor had gone back home. She left instructions for him to be monitored. But now he was lapsing into a coma. When they first arrived, Bobby had clung to him. "Uncle, don't leave me!" And he leaned over the side of his bed begging his uncle to hold him.

Now, he didn't know who he was, didn't recognize him. He was delirious.

Richard was frantic. He felt like the boy needed a father to protect him. He had no one. Richard needed him to be okay; he would lose it if Bobby died here. His patience wearing thin, he demanded that the doctor be called back. An hour later she arrived to see that Bobby's hands and feet were getting dark.

Richard shouted at her. "What is going on? Why aren't you doing anything? Can't you see he's getting worse?" She held up a journal. "We have the results from the spinal tap and I've been doing some checking. I think Bobby might have something called meningococcemia."

"What the hell is that?" Richard asked, staring at the pictures.

"It's a bacterium that invades the bloodstream. It can be fatal," she said as she pointed to the pictures of a kid with purple blotches on his legs. "And this is if they live," she said pointing to pictures of amputated limbs.

Richard felt like he'd been socked in the stomach and his knees threatened to buckle underneath him. He was furious. He whirled around and stormed out, his boots falling heavily on the tile floor. Then he whirled around and came back just as fast, arms pumping, yelling and, pointing.

"Are you kidding me? This is bullsh**! You don't know what you're talking about! You saw some pictures and think you know? You're wrong! I'm taking him to St. Francis in Wichita!"

"Mr. Lujano, calm down. We're doing..."

"You're not doing sh**! Your nurses are not doing sh**, sitting there with their feet up on the desk. We've been here five hours and now he's hallucinating! Get the release papers. I'm taking him the f*** out of here. Now!"

Richard stormed into Bobby's room and leaned over the bed. "Shooter, I'm getting Grandma and calling your dad. I'll be back." There was no response. Richard went to the nurses' station.

"I'm going home to alert the family. I want those release papers and an ambulance waiting when I get back!" He stormed out of the hospital.

Richard could not believe just last night they had been skating and having fun. The doctor was wrong. She had to be. But what if she wasn't? What if Bobby was really going to die? What would he tell his brother? He sped through town and ten minutes later he pulled into the driveway and ran to the front door.

LISA SAT ON THE BARSTOOL in the kitchen staring out at the cold through the window. She saw nothing in particular, nothing that moved. It was what she couldn't see that plagued her.

She'd had trouble concentrating in mass. She barely ate her lunch. What was taking her Uncle Richard so long to come home? Just then she heard his car in the driveway and he burst through the front door. He was pale and in shock, a look of desperation on his face. Grandma Hope's eyes grew wide as she stood up.

"Richard, thank God. We've been so worried. What's been keeping you?" she cried. "How's Bobby? The priest prayed for him during mass."

"It isn't good. We need to call Bob and get him back here."

"He was just here last weekend," she said, fretting.

"He needs to be here. It's serious. I don't know how to tell him."

They were oblivious Lisa was in the room. The seriousness of their words terrified her. It sounded like her brother was dying. They stood around the kitchen table, discussing a plan of action and then Uncle Richard picked up the phone to dial her dad's number. It was easy for Lisa to imagine her dad's words in between Uncle Richard's pauses.

"Bob, this is Richard. We had to take Shooter to the emergency room this morning. He's really sick."

How sick?

"Very sick."

What do I need to do?

"You need to come back as soon as possible."

Okay, let me wrap a few things up, get things covered at work and I'll head back in a few days.

"Bob, if you don't leave right now, you might not see your son alive again."

What? No.

That was it, the bombshell Lisa was afraid of. *"I don't want my brother to die! Don't let him die!"* She screamed over and over and over again through uncontrollable sobs. She felt like dying herself. She wanted to die right along with him.

Bobby was the only person in her life she could trust and rely on to be there. She begged God, "Please don't take my brother away; he's all I have left. Please Lord, don't take any more of my family away, I won't have anyone." She was responsible for her brother when her mom abandoned them and then when her father left them at Granma Hope's. She felt like it was she and Bobby against the world.

Uncle Richard cupped his hand over his ear to hear his brother above Lisa's screams before hanging up. Grandma Hope began to cry and tried to console Lisa but it didn't work. They didn't have time to calm down or be rational. Bobby was dying and they needed to get to the hospital, fast. Grandma Hope called Father Riley to meet them at Bethel Deaconess and then called Aunt Mary to watch after Johnny, Paul and Willie. Lisa said goodbye to her cousins and hoped she could bring Bobby back home with her. Then they piled into the car and sped through town.

Lisa couldn't believe her eyes when she saw the condition her brother was in: pale, sweating, hooked up to all kinds of monitors and turning blue; it was all she and her grandparents could do to contain themselves. Lisa clung to Grandma Hope and they cried together at the end of the bed.

Father Riley went to the side of the bed and took out his vial of holy oil to give Bobby his last rites. Lisa strengthened her grip on Grandma Hope.

Father Riley touched Bobby's eyelids, ears, nose, lips, hands, and feet with the oil, each one in succession and each time he touched Bobby he repeated the same phrase: "Through this holy unction may the Lord pardon thee whatever sins or faults thou has committed."

Lisa watched as Father Riley wiped each place he had anointed with oil with a piece of cotton. He made the sign of the cross over Bobby's body.

"May Your blessing come upon all who are anointed with this oil, that they may be freed from pain and illness and made well again in body and mind and soul."

Lisa broke away from her grandmother and crowded in between the priest and the side of the bed.

"Shooter! It's me, Lisa, can you hear me? Are you okay?" she whispered into his ear. There was no response from Bobby.

"If you want him to here you, you'll have to speak a little louder," said Grandpa.

"Shooter! It's me, Lisa. Do you know who I am?" Bobby turned his head and looked at her. "Do you know me?"

"No." It came out as a whisper, the word not fully formed on his lips.

Lisa burst into tears. Her own brother did not recognize her. She was all alone. She wasn't sure how she would live without him.

Richard stormed through the door. "The ambulance is here. I just signed the papers. We have to go now." He was yelling, his movements quick and erratic. "I can't believe these people, they don't know sh**; sitting around with their heads up their a**es." He jolted back through the doorway of the room and yelled down the hall to the paramedics, "He's in here! Hurry!"

Lisa watched in horror as the paramedics rushed in along with some nurses and quickly unhooked the monitors from the wall, transferred Bobby to a gurney and wheeled him down the hall. Just like that, he was gone. The three of them stood there for a moment listening to Uncle Richard's boots pound fast and furious behind the gurney. In that moment of silence they shared the same prayer.

"Don't let him die, please don't let him die."

UNCLE RICHARD SAT IN THE front seat of the ambulance with the driver. Sirens blaring, they made their way out of the parking lot and into the streets. Two minutes later, on Main Street in Newton, the window to the back section opened and the paramedic taking care of Bobby motioned to the driver, who pulled over and turned off the sirens.

"What are you doing?" Richard yelled.

The paramedic in the back said, "I'm sorry, but your nephew has expired. There's no need to go on to Wichita."

Richard flew into a rage. He couldn't lose his nephew. He wanted to punch the guy, but instead he and the driver both got out and went to the back of the ambulance. The freezing air went unnoticed as he yanked open the doors.

There was Bobby, dead, on the gurney.

Richard put his hands on his head, his eyes bulging from their sockets; he couldn't accept what he was seeing. His mouth flew open but no sound emerged. The two paramedics in the back looked at Richard and the driver in a helpless, deer-in-the-headlights, sort of way. Richard caught his breath and began crying and screaming all at the same time. He was hysterical.

"You," pointing to the guy on the left, "get those paddles and you jump start him, shock him, get him going again!" The paramedic immediately did as he was told. He readied the paddles, Bobby jolted, and the medic checked the machine. Nothing. He readied the paddles a second time, Bobby jolted and they waited. A weak heartbeat registered and he nodded at them. "You," Richard said pointing to the driver, "get back behind the wheel and get us to Wichita!" A look of fear passed the guy's face but he quickly did as he was told. They got back in the truck and flew through the town, speeding the twenty minutes to Wichita. Richard cried, unable to stop the whole way there. "Please don't let him die, please don't let him die, please don't let him die."

There was a team of doctors waiting for Bobby when they arrived at St. Francis Hospital. Dr. Rennebohm had been briefed over the phone by the doctors in Newton: this boy was in bad shape. In all likelihood, he was going to die. The sirens came screaming into the emergency room parking lot and the paramedics rushed Bobby into the hospital under Uncle Richard's watchful eye. They burst through the entrance like a crashing wave. The team in the lobby flew onto the gurney as if pulled in by a magnet.

"We lost him on the way here. We resuscitated, but he's barely hanging on."

"Put him in room 3."

The parade of people rushed down the hall. Richard did his best to keep up before being stopped outside the door.

"Are you the father?" asked a man in a white jacket.

"No. I'm his uncle, Richard Lujano."

"Where are his parents?"

"His mother left them some time ago and his father, my brother, lives in Texas. He's getting on a plane and should be here in a few hours. Please save him, please don't let him die."

The man noted the look of disbelief and panic on Richard's face. He put out his hand to reassure him.

"I'm Dr. Rennebohm. We'll take care of him."

Richard took Dr. Rennebohm's hand and looked him straight in the eye with fear, searching the doctor's eyes for some sort of affirmation, some sort of assurance that his nephew was not going to die...permanently.

"What does he have, is he going to make it?" asked Richard. He held the doctor's gaze a little too long and squeezed his hand a little too tight. He needed to let go, needed to surrender Bobby to the doctor. There was nothing else Richard could do. He had to let go.

"I need to go take a look at your nephew. This is a very serious situation, every minute counts. My first concern is to get him stable."

Tears welled up in Richard's eyes and with one final powerful shake he let go and backed away. He took one more look over the doctor's shoulder, into the room where the staff was working quickly to plug in the monitors and attach them to Bobby's decaying body. He prayed to God it wouldn't be the last time he saw his nephew alive.

"We'll do everything we can to save his life," said Dr. Rennebohm, and he turned and left Richard standing there, helpless and scared.

Richard needed a drink. Bad. He'd only been sober a short time and was still new to the AA program. With nothing else to do but wait, he started down the hallway, looking for something, but he didn't know what. Something to drink, something to eat, someone to punch. No one better get in his way. Defeated, he came across a waiting area and crumpled down into a chair putting his head between his hands, eyes closed. He was too numb to cry.

"Jesus wept."

John 11:35 NIV

4

Change of Identity

THE NURSING STAFF WAS SILENT but speedy as they plugged Bobby in to the monitors and started the IV. The only time they spoke was to give an instruction or to acknowledge one. No one knew what to say. The lifeless child on the gurney in front of them was a mess. He was purple and blue. A kid shouldn't look like that. A kid shouldn't die like this; or at all, for that matter. He should be running around, cracking jokes with his friends. The futility of trying to save him was like a black cloud pressing heavy on their shoulders. No one voiced it—they worked furiously to save him—but the vapor of doubt passed from nurse to doctor to technician and hung in every corner of the room.

As they worked, Dr. Rennebohm noted the terrible state the child was in: "Bob Lujano, nine years, six months old, delirious, septic shock, disseminated intravascular coagulation, myocardial depression, purpura fulminans." He looked at the nurse. "This is a classic case of fulminant meningococcal sepsis. We're going to pump massive quantities of fluid into him along with massive doses of antibiotics to reverse his shock and to increase blood flow to his extremities. Every minute, every second, is crucial."

Their looks were grave. They knew this wasn't likely to work. Only the doctor had seen this before. And it wasn't good. He remembered an article in a journal he'd read recently: "No other infection so quickly slays." The man who'd said that was W. W. Herrick, in a report from quite a few years ago, 1919 if he remembered correctly.

35

Dr. Rennebohm bemoaned that despite all the progress in medicine, some 60 years later it was still such a potent, lightning-fast killer. He was working against the clock. The invasion normally progresses to death within the first 24 hours.

When Bethel Deaconess Hospital called with the patient transfer report, they indicated the symptoms had started late last night. Dr. Rennebohm noted the time. It was 4:00 p.m. Roughly eighteen hours had already passed. He was at a clear disadvantage. He was fighting a bacterium that was literally eating this boy from the inside out.

The statistics were even grimmer. Very few survived, and those that did...

He had to push that thought out of his mind.

First things first. Keep the heart from succumbing to the shock.

He went to work. After a few hours, a nurse poked her head into the room. "Dr. Rennebohm? The boy's father has arrived. He's asking to speak to you."

She stood in the door and waited for a response. Dr. Rennebohm surveyed Bobby, the monitors, the nurses. Bobby was holding on for now. "I'll be right back." Those in attendance looked apologetically at the doctor and he went to face the father.

AN HOUR EARLIER, AS THE plane began its decent, Bob Sr. stared out the window and searched the ground below for St. Francis Hospital. He scanned the tops of the buildings, looking for the helicopter pad. His son was down there somewhere. His brother had been adamant, *Don't drive! Take a plane! If you don't get here soon, you might not see your son alive again!*

The sound of his daughter's screams through the phone had stiffened him. *Don't let my brother die! Don't let him die!* Those words rolled around in his head as he wondered if his son might already be dead.

But how? What illness could he possibly have contracted?

There was no understanding it. Richard wasn't helpful. He'd had no information. The doctor hadn't told him much and what he did tell him made him so mad he couldn't think straight. His brother was a hothead, but Bob knew Richard cared for his kids as if they were his own. Whatever was going on down there, Bob would get to the bottom of it. He would find out why his son was completely healthy one day and clinging to life the next.

He should have been there. He knew his mother and father had been taking good care of his kids, and he needed the help, but still. He should have come for the weekend. As the plane landed and came to a stop in front of the gate, Bob suddenly felt claustrophobic. It took too long to open the cabin door; it took too long for the people in the aisle to collect their belongings; it took too long for the passengers to say their goodbyes to the stewardesses. It was taking too long. *You might not see your son again.* As soon as he was free from the plane he ran through the airport to catch a cab to the hospital. He hadn't even bothered with luggage; all he needed was in his carry-on bag.

The family was there as he entered the waiting room in the ICU. His mother and father, his brother Richard, Lisa, the cousins, his sister Mary, they were all there. Many were crying.

"My son?" was all he could manage. He couldn't bear to ask if he'd made it in time.

"Thank God you're here," his mother said as she kissed his face several times.

He glanced at Richard who nodded. Bobby was still alive.

They all stood, hugged, kissed, and shook hands. Lisa squeezed him the tightest.

"Daddy, is Shooter going to be all right?" Lisa stared up into his eyes, waiting for an answer. He had never seen such fear and sadness in his daughter's face. All he could do was hug her and kiss the top of her head.

"Richard, where is the doctor? What's going on?"

"I've already told him you're here. They said he'll be out in a minute."

A few minutes later, a tall, thin man in a white coat came through the door. He approached and put out his hand.

"Mr. Lujano? I'm Dr. Rennebohm."

Bob Sr. sized-up the man in front of him as they shook hands. He had light brown hair, receding hairline, high forehead, and wore glasses. Something about his nondescript face put him at ease. Dr. Rennebohm carried his young features with a quiet confidence. Shooter's life was in this man's hands. Bob Sr. was immediately grateful yet felt helpless. He had to trust this stranger with his son's life.

"Can I see my son?"

"Of course."

Richard and Bob Sr. followed the doctor down the hallway. When they entered the room in ICU, Bob Sr. could not believe what he saw. There were monitors everywhere. Large portions of his son's body were purple and blue as if he'd been beaten within an inch of his life. He was on life support.

"I'm here Bobby," he said. "Dad's here." He turned to look at the doctor, "Can he hear me?"

"Your son is in coma."

"What's going on? What does he have?"

"Your son has a bacterial infection within the bloodstream called Fulminant Meningococcal Sepsis, or FMS. It is a rare form of meningitis." Bob Sr. looked confused so the doctor continued. "Your son is in septic shock, which means his blood is toxic with the bacteria and his pressure is dangerously low. The bacterium moves very quickly, damaging and blocking the blood vessels. When the vessels are damaged, the oxygen and nutrients can't get through. The purple blotches are where his skin has started to die."

Bob Sr. blinked and shook his head. Dr. Rennebohm paused to let him catch up. The heart monitor tracked a weak heartbeat. Richard shifted in the background, his boots squeaking in the silence.

Bob took Bobby's hand and looked at the doctor. "What do we do?"

The doctor continued, "The blood vessels massively dilate to get oxygen to the skin, but they can only do so much. Eventually they tear and blood begins clotting internally, which prevents adequate blood flow to the arms and legs, particularly the hands and feet. The skin and deeper tissues, muscle and even bone can die from lack of oxygen. When this happens..."

Bob Sr. whipped his head from Bobby to the doctor. "What are you saying?"

"I'm saying that this is serious. His heart is working hard and weakening, further lowering his blood pressure. Blood is leaking out the vessels. Soon, body tissue and organs will be affected."

Bob Sr. put his head onto Bobby's shoulder. He could hear the shallow breath coming from his son. Shooter was dying right before his eyes. It was just a matter of time. Was this it? Was God punishing him for something? He felt his own breath being sucked right out of him.

"What can you do to save him?"

"We already have nutrients and antibiotics trying to reverse the shock and keep blood moving to his extremities." Dr. Rennebohm paused.

"What are his chances?"

The doctor swallowed. "I don't like to answer that. I'm confident in the medicine and the science, but some things are out of my control. How much fight a patient has, how much inner strength they start with, and how much is still there to draw upon during the long recovery process."

Bob Sr. couldn't let it go. He knew his son's strength. "What are his chances?"

The doctor looked away. "About 10%."

Bob Sr. felt his knees buckle. This couldn't be happening. A father should not have to watch his child die. He imagined him on the baseball field, sliding into a base, diving to catch a ball. He'd wanted to make the big leagues and he'd been working all this time just to give his kids a chance.

Bobby was one of the best players on the team. Maybe if they fixed him, he could still play. He could still become the next Pete Rose. He couldn't imagine life without his son. He wouldn't.

"Isn't there anything else you can do?" pleaded Bob Sr.

"There is. But I would need your written permission. There is an experimental drug that could keep the tissue in his arms and legs alive, but the drug could also kill him. It's very powerful."

Bob Sr. choked back the tears.

"We are doing everything we can to save him. It will all depend on your son and how he responds to the medication. But if we can't get the blood flowing to the hands and feet, we may have to amputate. This medication could prevent it."

The blood drained from Bob senior's face and he began to sob. He couldn't listen anymore. It was too much.

"What about a second opinion?" said Richard.

"You're welcome to get one. I can get you the number to the leading specialist in the country. He's in Phoenix."

"Give him the drug," Bob Sr. said. Do whatever you need to do to save him." He leaned over and covered his son's body with his own, gently hugging him, his face buried in Bobby's neck. "Don't leave us. Don't leave us," he pleaded.

Richard stepped in and Bob collected himself. They walked back to the waiting room. Bob sat in a chair, dumbfounded, staring at the door that led to his son's room. He couldn't make sense of what was happening. It paralyzed him.

Richard couldn't sit still. He still needed a drink. He put his energy toward tracking down the nurse to get the number of the specialist in Phoenix. He finally got it and listened intently to the voice on the other end of the phone:

"There is no need to bring your nephew to Phoenix. Even though Dr. Rennebohm is currently an intern, he knows what he's doing. He is the second best in the country in the area of meningococcemia. You are in excellent hands. Rest assured you are getting the best care available."

When Richard heard that, the calm assurance it carried, his entire outlook changed. He knew: this was divine intervention for sure. To have this doctor on duty the day Bobby was brought to the hospital, the very hospital where this doctor was interning?

Richard couldn't help but tear up. He relayed the information to the family as he stood up and sat down, pacing back and forth. Grandma Hope made the sign of the cross several times across her chest as she wiped her tears. Grandpa Bill crossed his arms and rested his head against the wall. Aunt Mary cried. Lisa cried when Mary cried.

Minutes turned to hours and most of the family went home to wait. Within days, Dr. Rennebohm's medicine was able to reverse the shock, but Bobby's lower legs and feet were dying. The bacteria had caused too much damage; gangrene was setting in. Amputation was necessary. Bob Sr. was needed to give permission but he couldn't do it. This wasn't something he wanted on his shoulders; he didn't want it to be his decision.

How would he play ball? If he lost a few fingers, then maybe... maybe he could still throw. But his legs? How would he run the bases without legs? He couldn't bring himself to make the decision. He tried to put it off but there wasn't time. Bobby's life depended on a decision right now; a good, sound decision.

"Mr. Lujano, I really need you to give your consent," said Dr. Rennebohm.

"Is there any hope? Can't we wait a little longer? It's only been two days," he said.

"The longer we wait the more chance the bacteria from the gangrene will take over and he'll die. We need to amputate to save his life."

Bob Sr. swallowed hard. *Dear God,* he thought. *I can't do this. How will Bobby handle this?* He stared hard at the doctor. He looked around at the nurses sitting at their station and expected to see every activity come to a grinding halt. The world was changing but nothing was changed. The nurses were still going about their business. And why shouldn't they? Sickness and disease were routine for them. This couldn't be happening. He covered his face with his hands and walked in circles.

"Mr. Lujano? Please. We need to save your son."

He had no choice but to give consent. It was his son's legs or his life. What kind of decision was that?

"Okay. Do what you think is best," said Bob in a whisper, wrapping his arms around himself. Forms were brought and he carefully signed his name on them, his hand shaking and the walls bending in on him.

No one but the family could feel the weight of that simple signature scribbled down in anguish. Phones rang in the background. People played cards in another part of the room.

The doctor sped down the hall to prepare for surgery. The room began to spin.

Richard came up behind Bob and put his hand on his shoulder. "Come with me." The two men walked down the hall to an empty seating area and sat down.

"You really need to cry, Bob. Let it out. Other than with Bobby, you've barely spoken or shown any emotion since you got here."

"I can't. I have to be strong for Shooter."

"You need to let it out. Be angry, yell, cry, something. It's not good to hold it all in. Bobby needs you, but he needs you to take care of yourself. Let it out!"

Bob put his head back and stared up at the ceiling. He couldn't look at his brother. He couldn't accept any of this, let alone talk about it. He was in shock, but he was also angry. So very angry.

He turned to Richard. "How will he live like this? Huh?" He swallowed, staring into his brother's eyes. *"How will he live?"*

And with that, sobs began flooding out.

"I don't know," Richard said, putting his arm around him. "I don't know. But we will take this one day at a time, all of us together. You don't have to do it alone."

Bob spoke through his hands. "How could this happen?" He looked at Richard. "How *did* this happen?"

"I wondered that too. They were at the roller rink Saturday night. I picked them up, everything seemed fine. We went to bed and the next morning Mom woke me and told me to take Shooter to the ER. Paul said he was up all night with him. The fever and the spots started before any of us knew it. The nurses said they're checking in Newton for other kids who may have it. It's contagious, spreads through saliva. It could be an epidemic," said Richard.

Bob couldn't believe what he was hearing. A contagious disease from roller-skating? "Has anyone been brought in?" he asked.

"I haven't heard anything yet. The nurse said it's possible for someone to be a carrier but not contract the disease themselves. There are antibodies in the back of the throat that help ward off the bacteria, but sometimes it doesn't work. It must've had Shooter's number."

"Were they sharing food? Drinks? Why don't the cousins have it?" asked Bob.

"I don't know. It could've been from the drinking fountain. Anywhere."

THE FAMILY WAITED SILENTLY FOR the surgeon to return with news. Not much light came in through the small window. No one looked at each other.

Lisa sat beside her dad, trying to be brave for him. "It's going to be okay, Dad. It's going to be okay."

Bob put his head in his hands and wept.

No one left the waiting room that night. The family stayed, huddled in shock, doing the only thing they knew to do: pray. They prayed all night, petitioning the Lord for Bobby's life.

Lisa laid her head on the arm of the chair, her prayers turning to dreams as she slept.

BOBBY LAY MOTIONLESS IN HIS bed. The only sign of life for the past two weeks were the sounds of the monitors and IVs. Three days after the amputations, Bob stood at the window in Bobby's room watching the wind scatter the snowflakes. Lisa sat in the chair beside her brother's bed, keeping watch over the monitors.

Bobby stirred.

"Dad? He's moving," said Lisa.

Bob whirled around and gently called his son's name but got no answer. He was probably too full of pain medication.

"Bobby? Bobby?" he said again, this time closer to his ear. "Are you sure you saw him move?"

"Search muffett," Bobby slurred.

"Say it again, son."

This time it was clear. "Scratch my feet."

Lisa looked up at her dad and watched him go white as a sheet. He reached down and moved his arms pretending he was scratching Bobby's feet.

"Better?" he asked.

"Again," Bobby said, his eyes still closed.

Was Shooter really awake? Did he know what was happening? Lisa couldn't tell if he was delirious or if he simply didn't realize he had no legs. She wanted to run to the bathroom and vomit. Her dad remained calm and moved his arms again like he was scratching Bobby's feet. And then he grabbed on to the handrail and clung to it for dear life.

How brave he is, Lisa thought. She knew he would have to tell her brother that his legs were gone. And she could see in his face that he was pondering that very thing: what words to use to explain the nightmare?

But Bobby had fallen back to sleep.

The conversation could wait.

THE NEXT FEW WEEKS WERE a blur. Bob Sr., Uncle Richard, and Grandma Hope took turns staying at Bobby's bedside. Dr. Rennebohm had not left the hospital since Bobby arrived. His wife brought him food, but he refused to leave and take time off even to sleep in his own bed. Then there was more bad news.

"Mr. Lujano," said Dr. Rennebohm, approaching him in the hallway. "It's time we made a decision about Bobby's arms."

Bob Sr. didn't want to hear any more bad news. Amputate his son's arms? What would be left of him? He stood outside his son's room in the ICU, staring at him through the glass. Bobby's face and torso were blue and purple, his arms were black. He was dying. How could he tell his son he was giving permission, yet again, to remove his body parts? How could he make this decision? What kind of life will he have? He felt the weight of the illness, the weight of his decisions pressing hard on his shoulders. They had already taken a few fingers and his legs, he could still throw a ball. But as he looked at Shooter's black arms, he couldn't deny what must be done.

Maybe this was his fault. If he would have kept the kids with him, maybe this wouldn't have happened. If he hadn't taken the kids to his mother's house; if he'd just tried a little harder to handle things.

No. He wouldn't allow himself to go down that road. His wife abandoned them and he needed help to take care of his kids. His mother, Grandma Hope, was doing a fine job, as was his brother and sister. He was grateful to them. *Things happen. That's just the way life is. Things happen.* It was nobody's fault.

There's nothing you can do about it except move on. Just keep moving.

"Mr. Lujano?" Dr. Rennebohm called his name again.

He turned to face him. "Yes, I'm sorry, I was just hoping we didn't have to have this conversation," he said angrily.

"Believe me, I wish we didn't either, but we must. Gangrene will set in soon in Bobby's arms if we don't amputate quickly." said Dr. Rennebohm.

"And what will we amputate next, doctor? Huh, what next? His ears? His face? His chest? His whole body is turning blue! Will we just pick at the body parts until there is nothing left?"

Bob Sr. turned back to look at his son through the window, his hands high on the glass, pushing against it as if to make it all stop. After a slow exhale, he turned back to the doctor.

"I'm sorry. I know you're doing what you can."

"You don't have to apologize." said Dr. Rennebohm.

Bob pondered the doctor's eyes. They were compassionate. So attentive. He was desperately trying to save his son's life, chasing this evil bacterium from one body part to the next.

"Where do I sign?"

Bob signed the consent form and then walked to the side of his son's bed. He sat on the edge and put each hand on either side of Bobby. "Shooter? Shooter, can you hear me?"

Bobby opened his eyes.

"Shooter, I need to talk to you. Are you awake?"

"Yeah."

"Son," he said with a long pause, "you need to have another surgery."

"When did I have surgery?"

"Ten days ago. They amputated your legs. Remember?"

"No. They itch. Can you scratch my feet?"

Bob felt a wave of tears coming but he needed his son to understand what was happening. "Bobby, the medicine isn't working fast enough. We need to amputate your arms."

"WHAT?!" Bobby was suddenly fully alert and terrified. "Daddy, NO! Please! Don't let them take my arms! No, Daddy!"

In that moment, Bobby looked down and saw that his legs were gone. *Gone!* Shock set in as he tried to comprehend what his eyes were telling him. His thoughts immediately turned to baseball, the thing he clung to that brought him joy amidst all the pain. Pictures flashed in his head of sliding into home plate, running the bases, his dad cheering.

He cried, wracking sobs that left him shaking.

Bob Sr. tried to calm him down.

"I already can't run the bases," Bobby pleaded.

Bob tried hard to keep it together but it wasn't working. He was in pain, too. A nurse walking past the door put her hand to her mouth as tears filled her eyes. Bob put his face to his son's.

"Son, we have to do this. We don't have a choice."

"Yes we do! You can say no! Please, Daddy, don't let them take my arms!" he cried.

Bob choked and tried to gain composure. He stared hard into his son's eyes; tears streaming down both their faces. "Bobby, if we don't, you won't come out of here."

"What's going to happen to me? What will I do? How will I play baseball?"

Bob tried hard to be brave. He gathered himself and took a deep breath. "You won't be a normal boy. But you have to accept this challenge. You have to set your mind to what you want. This won't affect your brain or your ability to think, it's just a new challenge. Your life is *not* over. You are still young; you still have lots of opportunities. You can't just shut down."

That's not what Bobby wanted to hear. He cried harder and shook his head. "NO DAD! Do not let them do it! Do not let them take my arms!"

Bob leaned in closer, their noses touching. His eyes were wide and pleading. "Bobby. I don't want you to leave me. I want you to come

46

home. I want you to leave this hospital," he said, tears streaming down his face.

Something in his dad's voice caught Bobby's attention. He suddenly realized this was about more than baseball. More than his limbs. This was about living or dying. He saw his father's eyes and knew he had to choose.

He held his arms out in front of him. They were black.

"Okay, Dad. If you think this is what's best," he said, trying to stop crying and be brave like his dad. But he shook. He was so scared.

Bob took his son in his arms and they cried together.

GRANDMA HOPE SAT IN THE waiting room clutching her rosary beads and wracked with guilt.

Please, Father, save my grandson. Please forgive me. Please forgive me. I promise to take care of him for the rest of my life, no matter what condition he's in. Please forgive me. Please spare his life.

Lisa sat next to Grandma Hope: *Please, God, save my brother. He's all I have left.*

Uncle Richard paced the hallways, craving alcohol.

Please don't take him.

Bob Sr. sat in the waiting room next to Lisa.

Please, Father, don't take my son away.

Bobby waited in pre-op, praying,

Please, God, don't let me die. I don't care about my body. Just let me live.

DR. RENNEBOHM TOOK THE BRUSH, lathered it up, and scrubbed his fingernails, his knuckles, his hands, his arms. He'd scrubbed his pale skin hundreds of times for hundreds of different surgeries. But today, something felt different. There was an aura in the room that threw an anxious vibe, and he didn't like how it was threatening a cold chill in his spine. Certainly today this surgery was anything but, routine.

It occurred to him that doctors are supposed to save lives, not take them. He was suddenly plagued with questions as he unnecessarily began the scrubbing process all over again.

Am I taking Bobby's life by trying to save it? Am I doing the right thing? And what are we saving? Leaving him with no arms or legs? What kind of life will he have if he can't function on his own? Is it worth it?

A nurse poked her head into the scrubbing room, interrupting his thoughts.

"Dr. Rennebohm? We're ready for you."

"Alive, I'm Christ's messenger; dead, I'm his bounty. Life versus even more life! I can't lose. As long as I'm alive in this body, there is good work for me to do."

Philippians 1:21-22 MSG

5

Choosing Life

GRANDMA HOPE SAT VIGIL AT the end of Bobby's bed. He had awoken briefly after the surgery but was still delirious and feverish. As he slept in a somewhat comatose state, she noticed how small he looked in the big bed. A wave of regret flooded over her as she tried to make sense of the shock her body was feeling. Her grandson lay before her, practically an infant again and barely clinging to life. The beeps from the monitors were an annoying testament to how fragile he was.

If only I had gotten up sooner, she thought. *This is my fault. This is all my fault. I should have gotten up to check on him. I should have kept them home from the skating rink.*

Her thoughts plagued her with guilt and shame.

I will do whatever it takes to make this up. I will stay by him; I will take care of him for the rest of my life. Please, God, don't let him die. I promise to take care of him if you let him live.

Tears streamed down her cheeks as she pled for Bobby's life. She had to make this up to Bobby, and to God, if only Bobby could survive this terrible fate.

Bobby sat bolt upright in bed. His lips were moving.

"Bobby?" asked Grandma Hope. He looked like a miniature mummy, bandaged, bruised, blood seeping through the gauze.

Bobby was like a zombie, sitting upright, his eyes distant.

"Bobby? Who are you talking to?"

Grandma Hope could barely hear her own voice. A wave of panic froze her body in the chair.

"I'm talking to Jesus. I'm telling him to leave me here because I have things to do."

He sat, mumbling, his eyes locked on someone she could not see. Then he lay back down on the bed and closed his eyes.

"Bobby?"

Grandma Hope looked around again. The monitors continued their slow, steady beeps. Nothing in the room had changed. But a chill filled the air and she instinctively clutched her Rosary. She scanned the room holding her breath, searching for something to explain what just happened. She saw nothing but stillness.

Something bigger was going on, something beyond her control.

She made the sign of the cross and began to weep.

I REMEMBER VIVIDLY THAT CONVERSATION with Jesus, even though I was comatose at the time. He stood at the end of my bed and gave me a choice.

"Do you want to stay and live or would you rather come home with me?"

"I want to live. I have things to do," I told him.

There was no doubt in my mind, no hesitation, even though it would have been easy to die that day. From the day I got sick to the time in ICU after I was declared a quad amputee, it was all such a blur. There are very few things I remember, not much pain during that time and not much awareness other than the day I begged my dad not to let them cut my arms off.

Dying in surgery or asleep in the ICU would have been the perfect way to go. Just slip into paradise away from all the tragedy I had experienced in my nine years on earth and not have to deal with a battered body the rest of my life. But somewhere in that comatose state, I do remember making it clear that I wanted to live.

I did not have clarity that day about the things I had to do, but God in his goodness put a yearning in me towards the hope that life might be more than what I had experienced so far. I had some hurdles to get over first, brutal life lessons, but the fight in me to keep moving forward was strong from the beginning.

And somehow I was assured, despite all appearances, I had things to do.

"But we also glory in our sufferings, because we know that suffering produces perseverance; perseverance, character; and character, hope. And hope does not put us to shame, because God's love has been poured out into our hearts through the Holy Spirit, who has been given to us."

Romans 5:3-5 NIV

6

Healing

I SPENT 45 LONG DAYS IN the ICU. I looked like a newborn mummy completely wrapped in bandages. The ability to walk, run, brush my teeth, feed myself, go to the bathroom on my own…it was all taken away. My dreams of playing professional baseball were gone. I was a baby again needing constant care and attention. The bacteria continued their mission to destroy what little was left of me. It began eating the skin on my chest, my face, my lips, my teeth, my back, my ears, and my buttocks. The small areas of flesh on my body not affected by the bacteria were grafted off to cover the open areas and amputations. I was much like a burn victim with large patches of seeping flesh on every part of my body.

And the dressings had to be changed daily, so they sent me to the burn unit.

The process was the same each time: I was put into a net and lowered into a chemical bath, which made me scream in anguish. Once the bandages were soaked, they were removed. It was easier to take them off when they were wet. Some of the new skin that had grown since the last treatment came off with the bandages, this couldn't be helped. Then I was brought out of the bath and wrapped once again in fresh bandages. The whole process was excruciating—the yanking of skin, the burning of the chemical on open wounds. I couldn't help but be hysterical from the pain that came from somewhere so deep I only wanted to lash out. The nurses had to put a cover over my eyes to remove the bandages because I would completely lose it seeing the bones and cartilage hanging out in my arms. There was barely anything left and it terrified me to look at it.

It was decided that my dad would accompany me to the sessions in the burn unit. But once he heard my screams and saw all the blood, he collapsed out cold onto the floor.

"I can't do this, Richard. You'll have to do it for me," he said to my uncle once the nurses got him up and back out to the hallway. "I'll pick him up and put him in the net, but once he's in the bath, you need to take over."

So, my dad and Uncle Richard were a tag-team in the burn unit. I didn't like the man who was in charge of removing my bandages. He was rough with me and his personality was a little scary. I hated going to see him.

"Uncle, I want you to remove the bandages. I don't want that man to do it." I said.

"What? You don't mean that, Bobby," he replied.

"Yes, yes, I do. He hurts me too much; I want you to do it," I pleaded.

"I just don't think I could handle it, Shooter."

"Yes you can. I want you to do it. Don't let that man do it."

The nurse just stared at my uncle. "What are you going to do?" she asked.

"This treatment is hard enough to watch, let alone participate in. I can't be a part of causing you more pain," said Uncle Richard.

"You won't uncle. It'll be fine. I want you to do it."

With a long pause and a big sigh, my uncle relented. "Put a gown on me," he said to the nurse. And he began the tedious process of snipping the bandages and being ever-so-careful with the newly-formed skin. I was so grateful. He was much gentler than the man. And the visits were just a little easier from then on.

Back in my room, I was restless. "Uncle, pick me up and turn me. I can't stand to be on my back anymore." Uncle Richard picked me up but he lifted me too high; blood oozed out from under the bandages and down my uncle's arms. He was horrified. I tried to console him but it just made him cry.

"Don't worry, Uncle, it's all right. It's going to be alright. God let me live. It's going to be okay." He would tell me many years later that he was astonished and ashamed that I was the one consoling him.

For six long months I endured fifteen plastic surgeries on my face, teeth, gums, and body, each time waiting for new skin to grow so it could be grafted and placed on the open wounds. It was a big deal when I was moved to a regular private room and was able to eat with metal forks and plates instead of having everything through an IV. I couldn't use them myself yet, but at least I was being fed real food with real utensils.

At first, my story caught local attention. The newspaper reported there were only twelve to fifteen cases of Meningococcemia per year and several papers followed my progress all the way through college. The local community began to rally around me and my family. During my illness, three Newton banks established funds and collected donations to help with expenses; random strangers held cake sales, dances and benefits that were attended by city officials and U.S. Representatives; the elementary schools raised money and there was even a guy who ran a marathon to raise money. I was so grateful people were making my recovery such a big deal.

National momentum took over after all three major television networks came to the hospital to do interviews. I soon received personal visits and pictures from Tony Hill, Hank Aaron, Al Grabosky, and several professional sports team pictures. *The National Enquirer* did a feature story, asking readers to send me cards and letters. I received 4,000 well wishes from all over the world. The list of senders included actor Hal Linden from "Barney Miller," TV personality Ann Jillian, pitcher Danny Darwin of the Texas Rangers, and many nuns who wrote that they were praying for me.

After six months, I finally left the hospital on June 1, 1979, a quad amputee. Hope was all I had left when I came home from the hospital; hope that I could in fact have a normal life, despite my condition. This hope was centered on Jesus; He let me live so now I expected Him to give me a life.

"What a God we have! And how fortunate we are to have him, this Father of our Master Jesus! Because Jesus was raised from the dead, we've been given a brand –new life and have everything to live for, including a future in heaven—and the future starts now! God is keeping careful watch over us and the future. The Day is coming when you'll have it all—life healed and whole."

1Peter 1:3-4 MSG

7

Hope and Blessing

AT NINE YEARS OLD, THE life I was hoping for was gone. I felt the despair, the loss of mobility and independence, I felt the loss of a dream, but I didn't know how to articulate at that time the confusion of going to sleep a future Pete Rose and waking up not being able to walk to a base or throw a ball.

Just like that, it was gone.

My nine-year-old brain couldn't process it. I just wanted to go out and play like before. I was grateful to be alive but I did not want to be taken care of like a baby. I didn't have a choice. I had no easy time adjusting to my new body and the reality it brought.

I couldn't do anything for myself at first so I tried not to dwell on it. I was happy to be back at Grandma Hope's with my sister and cousins and Brownie, our terrier. Grandma Hope welcomed me home with my favorite meal: tostados, fried drumsticks, and Spanish rice which she fed to me. I was able to hold and toss a Nerf ball and my Grandpa actually played with me after work, which was a first. Maybe he felt guilty for punching me? He always said I wore him out because I never got tired of playing.

The tension was still there in the house but not as noticeable. We were all glad I was home. Watching my cousins run out to the field to play ball was the hardest thing. I cheered and called the balls behind home plate, but on the inside I wished I could run the bases and slide into home plate like before. My cousins didn't leave me out, though. We wrestled in the grass and played sitting games.

Grams made good on her promise to take care of me by spoiling me rotten. She gave me 24-hour care. She cooked for me like I was a king, drove me to every doctor appointment, fed me, bathed me, dressed me, brought me games and toys, and loved me like her own. My father finally put a stop to it and was adamant I learn to dress myself. She didn't like to see me struggle with anything but my father insisted I be independent.

Hope was inadvertently being spread to everyone involved in my illness, including Dr. Rennebohm. He and his wife came for a visit to Grandma Hope's house a month after my release. He was so relieved to see I was happy and getting along. We played games together on the floor, took pictures, and enjoyed a meal together. We celebrated with him the news that he had decided to specialize in pediatrics, in large part because of my case. We were all so grateful to him for everything he did. We thoroughly enjoyed our time together. He was a great doctor, and I am forever grateful to him for not giving up on me.

Even though my heart had stopped beating in the ambulance and I was declared dead, even though I was brought to him barely hanging on by a string, Dr. Rennebohm treated me as if I had life left to be lived. He gave me all he had. He didn't leave me for two solid weeks, and then he was with me as much as he could be the rest of the six months. He gave me a chance to start over and I am eternally grateful. I tried to express this to him during his visit, as best as a young boy could.

I celebrated my 10th birthday in July that summer. It was a great day that will remain seared in my memory because of my dad.

Approximately 200 friends and relatives came to the park for my party. I think we were all surprised I lived to be ten, so everyone wanted to be a part of the celebration, including the local media. We played softball, hot potato, and had cake and ice cream. This was the first time the majority of the people there had seen me in my new body. It was my first introduction as a handicapped person, which was the word used back then. Everyone was polite and welcomed me, but they stared and hesitated in how to treat me.

My dad was great. He didn't cower, or make apologies, or act embarrassed. He put me smack in the middle of the games and handed me the ball. When the kids giggled at me, he laughed with them to show me to laugh, too. When they asked questions, he answered them. When they pointed at us, he waved back. When they stood back and hesitated, he pushed my chair right up to them.

"Stick out your hand Shooter and introduce yourself, shake hands just like before. It's up to you to make the first move and make them feel comfortable," my dad whispered in my ear as he pushed my chair through the grass to meet them. I wasn't sure how comfortable they would be shaking hands with my elbow, but okay. I did what I was told.

My first introduction to the world as a quad taught me several golden lessons that I took to heart: Make the first move. Laugh at yourself. And get in the game. This triad of lessons has paid dividends many times over in my life.

On the day of my actual birthday, my Grandma Hope and my dad flew with me to Chicago for an eight-month stay at the Chicago Rehabilitation Institute. I wasn't thrilled about leaving home again but I was excited that I would get to go to a Cubs game while there. Grandma Hope left her home to stay every night in the hospital with me. Our time spent together was a great comfort. It didn't make me forget about home completely but it did help me feel like I wasn't alone.

It was hard for her to go through the reality of my disease; changing bandages, accepting more surgery, and struggling with me through rehab. But she eventually got used to it and took care of me like a mother. What an amazing woman. She was my best friend, my shoulder to lean on. She was mother, grandmother, nurse, and other than God, my first example of unconditional love. She gave up her life to take care of me; partly out of guilt, partly as an excuse to get away from an abusive husband, but mostly out of love. And I am eternally grateful to her.

Hope also came in the form of prosthetic limbs. I was scared and a little depressed going in to rehab, not knowing what to expect. I had already been in the hospital for six months and I wasn't keen about going back in for another eight. I wanted to be with my friends and my family. But I knew I would always be dependent if I didn't go.

The first day was the worst. I had endured so much pain in the hospital in Wichita that as soon as I saw the nurse coming with the cart to take my vitals and draw an initial blood sample, I freaked out. The sight of the needle brought back the pain of every cut, poke, dip, and tear my body had gone through. I knew pain was coming and this made me scream and cry before the nurse even touched me and I continued the yelling and hysteria until she was done. It took several people to calm me down. When it was finally over, I remember telling God a dozen times, "thank you that I made it through." Somehow that day never leaves my memory.

Most of the patients there had spinal cord injuries and they were adults. I was different with amputations and I'm not sure they were equipped to handle my case. There were only two other kids; Tony was disabled and Mike was a burn victim. Mike and I were friendly because I was still being treated as a burn patient as my flesh continued to heal but I didn't see him as much as I would have liked.

The disease had done so much damage to my palate and lips that I had seven or eight teeth removed while I was there. I threw up once at the dentist's office because of my fear of needles and shots. I also endured more surgeries on my legs at the children's hospital there in Chicago. They needed to be further amputated for external skin issues and to fit the prosthetics. More needles, more IV's. Rehab was mostly pain and loneliness. One day I broke down and cried at the sheer enormity of it all. I just wanted to go home and be with my family. Grandma Hope set me straight.

"That's why I moved here with you, so you won't be lonely. And the staff is here to teach you how to eat and take care of yourself."

That dose of reality pulled me out of my pity party. She was my constant companion and cheerleader. We also had short visits to Aurora to visit extended family and those were great getaways from the constant agony of improvement.

I actually began to have fun once I realized that I was there to get my life back and not just to endure more suffering. Up to this point, everything had been taken away, but now the negative was about to turn into a positive. I hated being taken care of and longed to do everything myself so I worked really hard to do what they said.

Once I wrapped my brain around the fact that I could engage in what they were teaching me to get my independence back, there was no stopping me.

My first set of arms was a three "finger" device with a metal thumb; they were more like pinchers. I use a similar device today when I drive. A cable attaches to the metal thumb pincher, which attaches to a strap, and the strap goes behind my back, across my shoulders, and down to my other arm. There are rubber bands in the strap, so when I move my shoulders, the rubber bands tighten and loosen, which causes the hooks to open and close like fingers or pinchers. The rubber bands lose tightness over time and need to be replaced so I carry them with me all the time. In rehab, I learned to put the arms on and change the bands by myself.

I was also fitted with legs, but it didn't go as well. Each leg felt like it weighed 500 pounds! The 1979 version was awkward, cumbersome, and not a lot of fun. They didn't really bend; it was like keeping your leg straight and lifting weights with your hips to move forward. I didn't wear them very much and opted to use a power chair for a short time. The arms, however, were a huge success.

The combination of upper body strength and prosthetic arms gave me everything I needed to set me on my way to everyday life. I learned to tie shoes, button buttons, and zip zippers as part of occupational therapy. I gradually progressed to cooking, pouring things, and opening containers. I used the hooks in the kitchen to bake a cake, open bags, pour, fill, measure ingredients and put them in a bowl. Using the arms opened up a new world to me; to be able to pick up a pan, use a spatula, and cook something edible showed me that I would not need a 24/7 caretaker. This went on to personal hygiene. I learned how to brush my teeth, comb my hair, and later I could shave.

These basic tasks made me feel independent and normal. I also learned how to pick up items from the floor, like pennies, needles, pencils, anything I would need to retrieve in my daily life. I had to re-develop hand-eye coordination and dexterity by picking up blocks and putting them into the right shape. I did all these things as a toddler but had to learn them all over again with the hooks. I needed to get a feel for the size and shape of things, and to handle big items as well as tiny ones.

During one session, the therapists put a necklace on the floor and I had to pick it up and put it on. I couldn't do it very well because it was behind my neck but I adapted a way to lock it in the front so I could put on the necklace by myself. I learned to tie a tie and dress myself. We went through the whole gamut, cutting food, using a fork, a spoon, picking up a glass and drinking from it, carrying dishes, everything you could think of that any person who was ten years old would need to be able to do. I don't remember anything being too much of a struggle, except the necklace.

The proudest moment of all was the day I realized I would still be able to write my own name. That was almost taken away, too. I know who I am, but to be able to put down my signature, in my own descriptive handwriting, was huge.

All signs were pointing to independence and I couldn't have been happier. Because of this, I look at rehabilitation as a great experience. It was painful and lonely and sometimes depressing but it was also exciting because it gave me my life back. I wanted to learn everything. I wanted to be independent and rehab taught me how. What a blessing.

The best part of my stay in Chicago was the day I met Pope John Paul II. On October 4, 1979, 1.2 million people jammed into the streets and at Grant Park to get a glimpse of him. Grandma Hope and I waited in the cold for hours, shivering under blankets and drinking hot chocolate in the festive crowd. We befriended a police officer, Jim Zwitt, who was also saved from the brink of death when his battalion in Vietnam was ambushed and he was shot twenty times. Officer Zwitt moved us through the crowd to the platform where the Pope was to speak so we could be as close as possible.

As soon as he came out, the crowd went wild. People screamed and cheered and cried and jumped up and down waving their hands in the air. The Pope had an aura about him that radiated as spiritual, beautiful, peaceful, and serene. It was just amazing. He seemed very sensitive but powerful as well. It seemed as if he could pick up the phone and talk to God. There was no doubt this person did not look like any other person I've seen. He exuded a strong relationship with God. He came out and blessed the crowd.

"Long live the Pope! Long live the Pope!" the crowd chanted.

He started to walk down the platform and there I sat, at the end of the ramp, waiting for my own special blessing. He came toward us, me, Grandma Hope and Officer Zwitt, looking like he was making a beeline straight to me. I remember him just looking into my eyes. I sat in my wheelchair, anxiously staring back into his eyes. I will always have that vision of him looking down on me with a sensitive, serene demeanor, and with passionate, caring eyes. It was a surreal moment, almost as if God himself was looking into my eyes and saying, *It's going to be okay, Bob. You chose life through me and therefore I am with you always. You're going to be okay.*

It will forever be emblazoned on my mind, him looking down at me. He gave me a traditional papal blessing in Latin and placed his warm hands on either side of my face. What an incredible moment. I will always cherish that moment of validation. He was gracious enough to also bless Grandma Hope and give us rosaries, which I still keep.

Officer Zwitt called a month later and said a package had been delivered to the police station from Vatican City. It was a picture and a negative of the Pope blessing me! I keep it to this day, hanging in my office.

I was released from rehab, having learned how to take care of myself, and came back to Grandma Hope's house, in the spring of 1980. I had missed the end of my third grade year and the entire fourth grade year. We were thinking it might be the end of my education. Things were different back then. There was very little support, if any, for students with disabilities. In our current day we have a long way to go with public services, especially with the large number of veterans coming back without limbs, but back then any type of support system to the schools was virtually non-existent. The schools didn't have staff members who were specially trained to handle disabled students. At my Grandma Hope's, I was happy to be living in a home again with my family, but watching Lisa and my cousins go to school every day was hard.

One day there was a knock on the door and there stood Mrs. Elda Bachman. She had followed my story in the news and took it upon herself to volunteer to tutor me so I could catch up with my schooling. Can you imagine! She didn't ask for payment; she just wanted to offer her skills so I wouldn't fall any farther behind. My grandparents immediately set up the common area in the basement as a classroom and for the next several months she tutored me in every subject, including music and physical education. My family really encouraged me but it didn't take much to get me going. I was happy to be learning like everyone else. I also asked her advice about which college I should go to. She thought that was a funny question from "such a young lad," so she redirected me.

"For now, let's just concentrate on doing the best you can do with what's in front of you." Mrs. Bachman taught me the third and fourth grade that summer. I soaked it all in at warp speed and by the fall I was ready to join a regular fifth grade class. This was a banner achievement, to avoid being held back a grade.

Because of her, nothing was lost.

During that summer I was also practicing what I had learned in rehab in a real world setting. I was able to do almost everything on my own. When my father felt comfortable enough with my progress, he moved Lisa and me back home with him in Dallas. Grandma Hope came with us. She endured a lot of verbal abuse that summer when we returned from Chicago. Grandpa Bill was jealous of the time she spent taking care of me and let her know it. He pushed her around a little and that was enough for her to leave once again and make good on her promise to spend the rest of her life taking care of me. She had stepped in as my mom, and I was glad she came. And being able to see my father every single day was something Lisa and I looked forward to.

"Remember our word to your servant, for you have given me hope. My comfort in my suffering is this: Your promise preserves my life."

Psalm 119:49-50 NIV

8

The New Benchmark for Approval

THE FAMILY OF THE NEWLY disabled person has a lot of power over how the injured person will heal and develop. They can make it worse by enabling dependence, or they can make it better by allowing the person to struggle through independence like everyone else. I am so fortunate to have had the latter, even though it was not easy.

Home life was good at first because everything was new and we were settling in to a relationship with dad after being gone for four years. In the beginning we worked to establish normalcy and get me back into school. Then the reality of our earlier life came back that we needed to toe the line or face the punishment.

That fall, when my dad enrolled me in the fifth grade, there was resistance from the principal. He didn't want me at his school. My dad went to bat for me. This is the conversation that was relayed to me years later:

"He can't come to this school. You'll need to enroll your son into a special education school. We don't have the facilities here to handle him. Not only that, but he will be a distraction to the other kids. They will fall behind," said the principal.

"You're worried about the other kids? What about my son? Are you afraid to give him a chance? Are you going to close the door on him?" my dad asked.

"He probably won't be able to handle the curriculum," said the principal.

"There is nothing wrong with his brain," said my dad.

"Can he even write?" asked the principal.

"Yes. He cradles the pencil and he has hooks to help him handle the books."

"I don't know. I need to think about the welfare of all the students, not just your son. I can't have the whole class getting distracted."

"Just give him a chance. That's all he wants. Don't be the first to say no to my boy. If you get complaints, if he can't do it, then I will take him out. But please don't tell him no. Just give him a chance," said my dad.

Now do you see where I get it? It started with my dad. He can do it. Just give him a chance. Gotta love my dad.

But there's an important lesson here that I want to point out: My dad did not march into the school demanding special services, or any kind of special treatment, or insist that they hire extra staff to take care of me. He was simply asking the principal to enroll me as a normal student. Inadvertently, he was also telling me to act like a normal student. He didn't say that out loud, but that was the implication. *Go to school and do the work like everyone else.*

So the principal said, "Ok, we'll try it out on a trial basis only. Let's just see how it goes."

Now, from my perspective, everything went smoothly. The principal was nothing but nice to me. He even helped me in the bathroom until I was able to figure it out. My fifth grade teacher was also instrumental in starting the year off right. She pulled me aside before the bell rang and asked me if I was okay with telling my story, and if I would be comfortable answering questions about my illness. My dad had already paved the way for me to know what to say: "Of course!"

I'm so grateful to that teacher for the way she handled the whole situation. It could have gone badly. When I came into the class, she introduced me as a new student and then asked me to explain why my arms and legs were missing. After I told the whole story, she allowed the kids to ask questions. They were full of questions. I answered every one of them without hesitation. They all wanted to play with the electric chair, which I allowed, and they touched me all over. This early lesson was very instrumental in teaching me how to navigate situations I encounter on a daily basis.

Just ask and I'll tell you. It's much better that way.

The teacher asked for volunteers to help me get acclimated to carrying books and moving around campus. Every kid volunteered. I didn't fit into a regular desk with my wheelchair, so I had a table in the back of the classroom and in the cafeteria. My volunteer for the day got to sit with me at my personal table, which was a special treat for them. They also helped me carry my lunch tray until I learned to do it for myself. Bobby Haines became my special assistant. He felt so proud and so privileged that he came to school in a suit!

I relied on my prosthetic arms quite a bit that year. They played a significant role in getting along in the classroom, even as the perspiration poured off of me from the effort. I was able to turn pages in books by using the eraser of a pencil, I could write, erase mistakes, carry my books and my lunch tray, feed myself, play ball at recess. Basically, after the first few weeks of school, I could keep up with my peers and do anything they did.

Except for one thing.

I had been an altar boy back in Kansas and I was eager to return to my duties. My friend and I went to the altar together but it didn't go as I'd hoped; I had a regular chair with handles before I got my power chair, so he pushed me everywhere to perform the duties. When I look back it was probably cute and sweet but not how I wanted it to go. I wanted to do it on my own. I thought it was silly to be pushed around like a disabled person. I wasn't really doing any of the duties, just getting pushed. So I stopped doing it.

Even after I had my power chair or legs my days of serving as altar boy were over. My dad says it was because the priests didn't want me to be an altar boy because of my hooks but I don't remember that. I just remember being frustrated because I was being pushed around. I still attended services every Sunday and tried not to think about sitting and not participating. I knew God still loved me and had a life for me and I was going to live it.

In the summer between my fifth and sixth grade year, I went to a rehab in Dallas to get fitted for a new pair of legs to replace the heavy, cumbersome pair I received in Chicago. The new pair weighed less and actually bent at the knee so that I could get up and down. I didn't feel like I was walking on stilts anymore. I started off using forearm crutches to help me balance. When I began rehab, I had hooks on my arms, forearm crutches, and the legs. All four limbs were completely occupied, just to be able to walk. So the point of rehab during that time was to learn to walk with just one crutch to free up my left arm to open doors, pick up books, shake hands, increase independence, etc.

One of the lady's helping me woke me up every morning at 6:00 a.m. I didn't like waking up so early but she said to me, "Don't you want to get out of here?" So she came every day and had me walk to breakfast in addition to my regular walking session later in the day. This was extra work for her but I'm glad she went the extra mile.

Some of the rehab routines are boring; it's the same thing over and over again. If the rehab person does not have the passion to mix it up a bit, it translates to the patient. This lady was a blessing in her commitment to get me moving. It was a psychological boost; downstairs in the cafeteria the food was much better. It was exciting to eat there instead of in bed. My recovery went much faster. I had to walk and walk and walk to master those legs. I sweated my way through until I was able to walk out of the facility on my own.

At the start of my sixth grade year I actually walked to school! I wore a backpack to carry my books and was as independent as I could be. On the first day of school I felt very animated with all the stuff. I was a little scared. I hadn't figured out the routine yet. What was I supposed to do when I arrived at school?

I wasn't sure what to carry with me or leave in my locker. When the bell rang, I only had five minutes. When I finally walked into the classroom the teacher suggested that I have a helper. It was nice to have someone help me but eventually I grew out of it and no longer needed the help. I really wanted to do it on my own like everyone else.

When my illness took away the possibility of playing sports, I thought the possibility of winning my dad's approval was also gone. But my dad never expressed disappointment that he couldn't watch me on the baseball diamond anymore. He never complained that I couldn't participate in this sport or that. That really aided my emotional healing.

But as I look back on my early sports years, I have to be honest. My obsession with Pete Rose wasn't about Pete Rose, even though I enjoyed watching him play and wanted to be like him. My obsession to play baseball and be successful was to please my father. The love I have for sports in general was because he engrained it in me. Good or bad, I learned from him the importance of playing hard and giving it my all to be a successful player. This was an important lesson that would serve me well in my life. When sports were out of the picture, he quickly switched gears and became my academic advocate in many ways.

Still, the way he went about it made it a tough go for me.

When my report card came in, he'd get out the belt if I didn't make As and Bs in every class. One semester in the sixth grade I received three Cs. Some parents might have given the limbless kid a break. Learning to walk on prosthetic legs and use hooks and crutches to fit in might be enough. But not for my dad. I got the belt and I was grounded for six weeks—no phone, TV, music, friends. I was in my room with a book and could only come out for dinner. Six long weeks.

I got the point. I needed to take academics seriously. This was the new benchmark for approval. I didn't make any more Cs. I do remember my best and worst report card ever. I was in the seventh grade: three A+s, two B+s, and one F. In math. Obviously, I wasn't ready for the advanced class.

I knew I was in huge trouble. Lisa was good at duplicating my father's handwriting, so I tried to talk her into signing the report card and changing the F to a B. She wasn't crazy about the idea but I was adamant. I didn't want to be punished. In the end, I changed my mind and decided against it. I manned up and took it to him. His reaction still makes me laugh. He looked joyful, then sad, then happy, then angry. I thought he would go into cardiac arrest. He finally got a puzzled look and cursed, "Grades good except a *damn F!*" Through his confusion, he said I was grounded for a month. I was just glad this time I didn't get whipped. From then on, I earned A's and B's the rest of the way through junior high, high school, and college. And Lisa did the same.

What I didn't know at the time was that he carried a huge fear I'd be dismissed in the world. He was so afraid people wouldn't give me a chance. It was the first thing he honed in on in any new situation. He'd had to prove himself worthy many times on the playing field. And his dad, Grandpa Bill, as the only Hispanic, grew up sitting in the back of his all white church, continually proving he was worthy to be there. This is why he built his own church across the street after he married Grandma Hope. It runs deep.

I think my dad thought I would always have to live at home. He wouldn't have minded a bit, but deep down he was pulling for me to be a productive member of society as much as I was. In his mind it was all about wanting me to be accepted and able to provide for myself. He just didn't express it very well; the belt was the only tool he had to get me to perform my best so I wouldn't be dismissed.

With teachers and strangers, his fear came out as a fighting warrior on my behalf. "Are you going to give my boy a chance, or what?" With me, it came out as strong discipline so I'd toe the line and use everything I had to succeed. After my illness he had a new urgency. My brain and my personality were all I had left to try and make it in this world and he was determined that I do my absolute best. There was no more room for error. What was left of me had to be beyond excellent.

Besides the academics, school was a great place to get on people's good side and not get them upset. I am so thankful for the role prosthesis played in my social life. They helped me to be independent and participate in all school activities, including dances. I wasn't brave enough yet to ask a girl to be my date, but I went and had fun with a group of friends. Even though I wasn't the best dancer (nobody cared at that time anyway), I still had the courage to be on the floor and move to the music. I asked just about every girl there to dance with me and they all turned me down. This is how a person makes their way, doing what needs to be done.

I don't see it as rejection. I see it as character development. You have to go through a bunch of no's to get to a yes.

In PE class, I was told I couldn't participate with the able-bodied students. They wanted me to go to a separate room to play checkers. This is not acceptable to a guy who wanted to play professional ball. My passion to play didn't disappear along with my limbs. I still had a strong desire to compete. I did not want to succumb and suffer with my disability.

They brought in a counselor for limited exercises but I was still isolated from everyone else, so I took it upon myself to get back with my able-bodied peers. I began working out independently and then with friends. I threw the football back and forth with the counselor and this turned into a football game in the small room with the boys in PE. This was my first experience with able-bodied peers as a disabled, and their first experience with a disabled peer and seeing what abilities I had. The confidence between us soared. I made myself a part of the class. I didn't wait to be invited. I wanted to play with everyone else, so I did.

I got involved in basketball and soccer. I used the power chair for soccer but also had my crutch so they made me a defender to help the goalie. I couldn't kick but I could stop the ball with my crutch using upper body strength. For basketball, we played on the half-court so I stood in the middle without having to run up and down. When the ball needed to be blocked I stuck my crutch in the air. I was the tall person! During team selection I was one of the first people picked because with my crutch I was the tallest and could block the shots.

This was great for building camaraderie and showing my athletic skill. On days I didn't play on the court, I was the sideline referee or the scorekeeper; still a part of the action. The kids were not afraid of me because I was not afraid of me, and this made PE a very positive experience that I carried all the way through high school. I proved that I could be a part of the team, part of the able-bodied activities. I'm so grateful for this. Today I tell the kids I teach to get involved in PE. It's not social hour. Exercise is good for everyone.

At home I played tackle football with friends in the backyard. We also had a hoop in the driveway for shooting baskets. Sometimes I beat my friends, but mostly it was great to just keep up and have fun. Without the prosthesis I wouldn't have had these experiences. I would have been watching from the sidelines. I took it upon myself to push my way in. I realized it was up to me make myself a part of what was going on. I wanted a recreation experience and it was up to me to make it happen. I am so thankful people allowed it.

It was a challenging two years developing courage, confidence and independence, but from then on I carried myself forward; though not without struggles. Soon my Grandma Hope went back to Kansas because my dad remarried.

In all the time I've known her, she never said anything negative about anyone. She defended me when I needed it. She embraced me and cared for me in my greatest time of need. I am convinced that her affection and tenderheartedness is a result of her own broken childhood. She helped heal her own wounds by giving the love she so desperately needed as a child. Grandma Hope took us in and raised us like we were her own kids. No complaints.

When she returned to Kansas, she was finally brave enough to separate from Grandpa Bill. She had given so much to me and had received much in return; she was finally strong enough to realize that living with an angry, abusive man was unthinkable. It had gotten ugly and he finally moved out. But not before he'd beaten her up one last time. She couldn't divorce him because that would prevent her from taking communion at the Catholic Church so she was able to legally separate. I believe she'd gained strength from showing love and being loved in return.

Although her house had been chaotic, she never seemed to waver or lose her generosity or selfless spirit. Her actions and words always reflected kindness.

I will forever treasure the time spent and lessons learned from Grandma Hope.

"Honor your father and your mother, so that you may live long in what the Lord your God is giving you."

Exodus 20:12 NIV

9

Subordinate Son

I LED A VERY STRAIGHT AND narrow childhood through middle school and high school. Growing up with a fear of my dad kept me out of trouble. I was no different than any other kid. I had friends that showed me drugs and smoking and beer; it would have been so easy to take those paths because of the thrill of it and because I was young and didn't know better. But I didn't jump over the cliff because of the fear of disappointing my dad. He showed me that fear can be a great motivator.

But there was also love and compassion, for which I am thankful. Not the physical kind; he didn't start hugging me or telling me he loved me until I was close to thirty years old. The love and compassion came when strangers tried to dismiss me or tell me no. Dad was not going to have it. He fought for me to be accepted. He was proud to be with me in public, not ashamed. He told me not to get stressed or upset if people can't handle what they see. He took me right up to them and started a pleasant conversation if he saw them cower at my appearance. My dad's reaction became my reaction. I began to see people's reactions as no big deal. He taught me that I had to take the lead; it was up to me to be approachable and friendly. The way he handled these public interactions was so crucial to my mental stability that I am still reaping the benefit to this day. I try and pass these messages along any chance I get.

However, being his son meant accepting how things were under his roof. And when Dad remarried, dealing with a new stepmother on top of everything else was stressful. It was not a smooth transition. Grandma Hope left and our step-mom moved in. It was rough, but at least we had two parents who actually wanted to be there. My father was happy but family life doesn't always go the way you want it to go. Our step-mother was different than what we were expecting or hoping for.

She didn't make it easy for herself; she didn't fit the mold of a typical Hispanic woman. She put her foot down, spoke her mind, and had a fiery temper. You didn't want to be on her bad side. We thought it was up to her to adjust to our family, but she made it clear it was up to us to adjust to her. She doesn't take any static from anyone, doesn't cater to anyone, and she wasn't going to play the role of the passive housewife.

I had my ideas of how a person should be if they are coming in to fill the role of mother. I missed my Grandma Hope and my step-mom seemed like the complete opposite of a nurturing mother. But we have to let people be who they are. It's not our job to change them or complain about who they are, or to place our expectations on them. Our job is to love them anyway the best that we can. If people fit into our mold and behave the way we want them to behave, life would be a walk in the park. No struggles, no conflict, and no growth.

She is who she is and I chose to love her the best way I knew how. It was one of the most difficult things I ever did. There were words that she said and things that she did to me that upset and angered me but I had to let it go. They had two sons together, both of whom I love today, but early on they were her favorites and I was not. I was in my father's house and I did not want to make waves. I did not want to be the reason for another divorce. I chose to let things roll off my back so as not to cause discord between the parents.

I knew that one day soon I was going to leave and be on my own so I just took it all and didn't say a word. You could call this passive but because of the heavy discipline, I have no problem saying I was laid back; maybe to a fault. I wouldn't say I'm a pushover or a dishrag, but I will take the road that is easily traveled as opposed to causing rifts. I do know when to say enough, but sometimes it takes a while. In my father's house I did what I was told. I wanted to speak up but I was going to leave so why cause trouble? They provided for me and I wanted to show my appreciation. I didn't want to leave on a bad note.

However, there were many positives. If my back was against the wall, I could reach out to her. With her temperament and disposition, she would go through a brick wall for me and stick up for me. Conversely, if I was the one on her bad side, she might send me through the brick wall. So I tried to get along.

My dad was a great provider and was always at his best in making tough decisions. We were not spoiled but I never wanted for much. He is someone I can depend on; there is nothing he would not do for his family. I know I can call either of them at any time and they would help me in a heartbeat. I try not to abuse this. I take pride in knowing that over the last fifteen years I have only called once or twice for money. They offer whenever I am home but I always refuse. I take pride in that.

In middle school I started speech and debate. This class is one of the best things that ever happened to me. My confidence really progressed as I received many ribbons from the judges. During the same time period I took the teacher's daughter, Karen, to the dance. I was growing taller, alongside my peers, with each new set of legs. But it wasn't just physically, I was growing taller emotionally. Seeds were being planted to give me the emotional tools to be a successful adult male.

In high school I continued the speech and debate but didn't do so well in the girl department. My senior year I wrote and delivered an oratory titled "The Ultimate Challenge in Life," and placed in the top 15 in the State. I was also in performing arts and acted in a few plays. But the girls didn't want to date me. I always wore my legs at school and in front of girls but as soon as I got home I would take them off. As much as a blessing as they were, they were still cumbersome and it took a lot of energy to get around. One day, on the way home from speech and debate, I didn't feel like wearing them so I used my chair instead. Before I got into the car with my dad, I saw a girl that I really liked. She saw me without my legs, sitting in a wheelchair. I was really embarrassed and uncomfortable.

I was never taken seriously for dating. It was all about the jocks at that time and I was just a nice guy. I got along great with all the ladies as a friend but they wouldn't date me. I was just a sweet preppy nerd, wearing iZod's and getting A's and B's in all my classes.

I was still friends with Bobby Haines from elementary school. He was a lifeguard at the local pool so we spent the summers together, me swimming and him watching out for me and the other swimmers. He also got his first car at sixteen, a Beretta, so we cruised around town, met friends at the movies, and did what high school boys do. We tried to have a party at his house once but none of the twenty girls we invited showed up; it was six nerdy dudes, no girls, and a counter full of food. We were officially certified geeks.

However, we did have one redeemable moment our senior year. I really wanted to go to my senior prom so I selected a sophomore to be my date, Sonia Hernandez. Luckily, she said yes! We were both really excited. A week or two prior, she came and said she was reluctant about going because her sister was a senior and didn't have a date. Sonia felt bad that she was going to her sister's senior prom and her sister would be staying home. So I did what any real gentleman would do. I invited her sister to join us. I was going to the prom with two girls! Then Bobby called and said he didn't have a date. He had a limo, but no date. I told him I would share from my abundance. On prom night, we all piled into the stretch Mercedes and had the time of our lives. It was all harmless and innocent and the girls were great dates. We painted the town until two or three in the morning. What a great experience.

I was also giving serious thought about what I wanted to do with my life after high school. At the time, there seemed only one thing for me to do: enter the priesthood. Deep down, I questioned whether a woman would ever want to be with me in marriage. I had a hard enough time getting a date to a movie; I figured a lifetime commitment would be impossible. *Who will want me in this condition? Who will be able to put up with my disability?* The only person I could think of was God. By entering the priesthood I would serve Him and Him only. This would be my union, my wedding. I wouldn't have to worry about being rejected. God gave me my life; he proved he wanted a relationship with me, so I decided I would unite with Him in the priesthood.

I applied but was promptly rejected because I didn't have hands. I was shocked. I couldn't understand why the church was shutting the door. I didn't see it as a no from God; I saw it as a no from the church. Their reasoning was simple: hands are consecrated to consecrate others; the hands need to be anointed. It is written in their cannon laws and they say they have scripture to back it up; if you don't have hands, your hands cannot be anointed. I guess my elbows weren't holy enough. It wasn't an issue of serving or helping people, it was that the chalice and wafers were not to be touched with the hooks I was using; anointed hands only.

The news media was still following my story somewhat so it was out that I wanted to become a priest. The human rights people caught wind of what was going on and got involved. They wanted the Catholic Church to give me a chance. The church tested me, put me through the movements and I did okay but they were adamant that I not serve communion without hands. The human rights people threatened to challenge the church with legal action. They/we said that if I couldn't serve communion or be a parish priest, then maybe I could be a priest that helps other men become priests. The church had objection after objection. No way was I getting through that door.

There was one priest that was on my side. He said that if I really wanted to do this, I could go through the four years of seminary and he would fight for me when I graduated. But, becoming a priest is like getting married. I would be locked in. If I went through seminary and the church still did not accept me into the priesthood, then I will lose those four years of my life. The education to become a priest doesn't transfer to regular educational institutions. I would be taking a big risk. His advice to me was to go and get a regular four-year degree and then if I still wanted to become a priest, I could come back and he would fight for me.

Being rejected from the church, from the right to become a priest, was worse than losing my limbs in many ways. I was completely devastated. Vulnerability rose in my throat and choked me. If I couldn't be in union with God, then I would be at the mercy of the female population. Who would want me? I seriously doubted I would ever find a woman that could look past my broken limbs. This was hard to swallow. I went through a short time of depression. I tried not to let on that my heart was broken. I just wanted to blow it off. But it was hard not to show it. I prayed that God would still be able to use me as a servant to Him.

I graduated from Grand Prairie High School in May of 1988. It was a big event. Many of the extended relatives we hadn't seen in a while came for the weekend. My graduating class had 472 students. We used the football stadium for the ceremony and there were approximately 10,000 people in attendance.

Emerson Walls, the Quarterback for the Dallas Cowboys and one of my favorite players at the time, gave the commencement address. He wasn't supposed to make it to the NFL but did and became all-pro. I got to shake hands with him. I remember standing in line waiting to go up to the platform to receive my diploma. The families were allowed to yell for each graduate so as I waited I surveyed the stadium, wondering which direction their cheer would come from. I had no idea where they were sitting. When I walked across the stage and they announced my name, the entire stadium stood up and yelled! I was completely taken aback. It choked me up enough that I had to pause my steps to regain composure. I was just looking for my family and instead got a standing ovation from the entire stadium.

The people in the community had embraced me and understood my story. They followed each milestone I went through and were letting me know by this show of support. It was an emotional moment I will never forget. I felt so honored; it was so gratifying to know they would do that for me. I'm so grateful for that experience. It was a very important moment, no doubt about it.

That summer after I graduated, I was invited to be a guest on Regis and Kathy Lee. That was fun. They wanted to congratulate me on finishing high school and getting ready to enter college.

At eighteen I had a list of twenty things I wanted to accomplish in life. Among them were drive, have my own house, buy my own car, water ski, skydive, get married and have kids. Over the next several years, I began to check these off one by one.

"As water reflects the face, so one's life reflects the heart."

Proverbs 27:19 NIV

10

People who Stare

I FLEW TO BIRMINGHAM AND STAYED with Bob at his house for three days. I needed to see first-hand where he works and how he lives. What was his daily life like?

I had followed every lead, interviewed every family member, doctor, coach, and colleague. I read every news article written about Bob from the past 30 years and dug up whatever else there was to find like weather temperatures and football scores. Bob had already given me his story via recorded messages, and the 200-page manuscript was typed and tucked into my briefcase. But I didn't fully trust what I'd written. Travelling to Birmingham, I was after the *real* story. And maybe I was spying a little bit. I wanted to know if what I was told was really all there was. What really made him so unique?

What I found put me in a bit of an emotional conundrum.

Bob is a great host. His aura exudes grace, compassion, generosity, warmth; I soaked it all in. I loved just being around him. When I landed at the airport, he called me on his cell to tell me he would be parked in front of baggage claim. I tried to picture how he'd made the call while driving. He took me to Shooters for chicken wings. I had been with him before but never like this. Now I was on a fact-finding mission.

We caught up with small talk, how my kids and husband were doing, what was new with him, but I was preoccupied. I noted how he bit the paper off the tip of the straw, dropped it to the table and then held the straw in his teeth and pulled the rest of the wrapper off with his elbows. Equally impressive was the way he unwrapped the silverware from the napkin burrito by biting the paper string holding it together and unfurling the rest with his elbows.

Thank God for Dr. Rennebohm, I thought. He had the foresight during surgery all those years ago to leave a two-inch section of his forearm below his elbows so Bob has just enough to pick up straws, forks, pens and chicken wings. He puts the wing in his mouth, cleans it, and deposits the bones on his plate. The dexterity was incredible, like watching an Olympic gymnast, or a contestant on one of those obstacle course shows. On the way out of the restaurant he suddenly sped past me at warp speed, 0-60 before I could blink and slammed into the door with his chair to open it for me.

I was even more impressed. A true gentleman!

He lives in a two-bedroom duplex in a nice neighborhood. The driveway is at an incline to the house. His mailbox sits below at street level. No problem. He steers his car close to the mailbox, rolls down the driver's window, retrieves the mail, then pulls up to the flat section of the driveway as close to the house as possible. He bought the house new in 2009 and his sister Lisa urged him to have the contractors give him a flat driveway so he wouldn't have to deal with a slope in his wheelchair. He adamantly refused.

"It won't look good Lisa, to have one driveway in the neighborhood different than the others."

I put my foot in my mouth when I said to him, "Oh my, you're going to roll down the driveway!" I imagined if I was in a chair, I would roll down the slope trying to get out of the car.

"Will I?" he shot back.

His tone caught me and I realized what a dumb thing to say. He'd told me many times that he wouldn't put himself in a situation he couldn't handle. My remark was that of distrust.

He wears his car, house, and work keys on a lanyard around his neck. He wheels to the front door, uses his elbows to get the right key to unlock the door, and once inside switches to a different chair.

"Why do you do that?"

"The inside chair has clean tires. Keeps the carpet clean," he said, wheeling past me and giving me the grand tour.

The kitchen is decent size with standard height countertops, about the height of his shoulders. He keeps his everyday drinking cups, plates and silverware on the corner of the counter. "It's easier there." I asked him about the stick I saw him use in the movie *Murderball* to turn the faucet on and off. He reluctantly pulled it out from under the sink and showed me how he pushes or pulls to turn the water off or on.

The refrigerator was typical of a bachelor: empty. What was there sat on the lower shelves. The cupboards were the same; the lower cabinets contained the dishes and what little food he had and all the uppers were bare.

"Bob, there's no food in your house!" I laughed.

"I know. I was sick before you got here so I haven't been to the store in a while. I mostly eat out anyway because of my schedule. I can cook spaghetti, quesadillas, whatever I want, but it's quicker to grab something on the way home."

I just nodded and smiled, trying to get the visual of him navigating a pot of boiling water and pasta.

"Don't worry; I'm going to feed you while you're here. I won't let you starve!"

I laughed. "I'm not worried."

The laundry room contained front-loading units. The guest room "needs a bed" and the office has his computer. The living room is quaint with a brown couch and chair and the TV stand holds family pictures and mementoes. Everything was typical bachelor pad. Nothing in the house had been adapted and there was no special equipment anywhere.

"I hope you don't mind sleeping on the couch. It's comfy. The sheets and towels are in there," he said pointing to the hall closet.

As I fell asleep that night I wondered what I was looking for.

The next day, he took me to his office and I met his boss, co-workers, and the many patrons (all of whom love Bob) who come to The Lakeshore Foundation to participate in recreation and fitness programs. What an impressive place. It's a huge facility that has two indoor heated pools, three hardwood basketball courts with a 200-meter track around them, a shooting range, a 6,000 square foot fitness center, a research laboratory, community and conference rooms, a climbing wall, offices, and cottages for the injured military service men and women and their families who come to participate in the Lima Foxtrot program. There are also dormitories for U.S. Olympic and Paralympic participants when they come to train. There are eight tennis courts and buildings that house the HealthSouth Lakeshore Rehabilitation Hospital and the Birmingham Office of the Alabama Department of Rehabilitation Services (ADRS) as well as the National Center on Health, Physical Activity and Disability (NCHPAD).

When I sat with the president of Lakeshore, Jeff Underwood, he told me the mission. "We enable people with physical disability and chronic health conditions to lead healthy, active and independent lifestyles through physical activity, sport, recreation and research." I quickly realized every town in America needs a life-giving facility like Lakeshore.

Bob invited me to sit in on a couple of group rehab sessions he was leading. During the first session we sat in a circle, divided into two teams, and played bocce ball. I was horrible. In another session we played darts. Not good there either. Actually, none of us were a match to the high-functioning quad named Mike; he had his own professional darts! I asked him if this made for fair competition. Wherever he wanted his dart to go, that's where it went. He won every game by a landslide. Darts are not in Bob's skill set so he kept score and added up the points, neither of which are in my skill set. So I just kept trying to hit the board, while the other players added the obligatory smack talk and friendly camaraderie.

As the day wore on, I was beginning to unravel. I started to notice I kept saying *I can't...I'm not good at...I'm so uncoordinated ...I'm the weak link. You don't want me on your team...* Now I was embarrassed of my behavior. Here I was playing games with men confined to wheelchairs, quadriplegics, paraplegics, and I was being beaten and becoming negative and whining about what I couldn't do. The gentle ribbing had soon faded and not one of them complained about what they couldn't do! I was trying to "figure out" Bob, but my weaknesses were showing and it threw me off.

I hoped I wasn't embarrassing him. I was sure I was. Did I mention he is extremely gracious? I left that day feeling bad and defeated.

After work he took me for pizza and a movie. There was a family next to us at the pizza parlor, all adults that would not stop staring at Bob. I had seen him eat pizza before but they had not. He picked it up with the bend of his elbows, cradling it on the flat part of his left elbow. He made it look easy. Then he picked up his fork with both arms and stabbed straight down into the salad, somehow moving the bend in his elbows so that the end of the fork swung up to his mouth. I saw it with my own eyes and it still doesn't make sense. But the people next to us were bug-eyed.

Bob did what he always does when people stare: he looked right at them, smiled, and started a conversation. "Hello! How are you?" They sheepishly engaged and stopped staring. Bob's easy demeanor changed the mood on a dime; like taming an alligator.

We happened to leave the restaurant at the same time and said goodbye to the foursome in the parking lot. But as soon as they caught sight of me standing on the passenger side, they did not hide their incredulous expressions. *No way is that guy going to drive!* All four of them stood there, mouths gaping open, as he opened the door for me and I got in.

The next two minutes felt like ten. He wheeled to the back passenger side door, opened it and lifted himself up to the floorboard by holding his right arm on the door and his left arm on the seat and swinging his hips in. Then he reached down, folded his chair, and raised it in front of him into the space between the back seat and front passenger seat. He climbed onto the rear seat, reached to close the door, then climbed through the middle up to the driver's seat. He put his prosthetic harness around his shoulders, slid his elbows into the hooks, put his seatbelt on, turned the key and pulled out. We waved goodbye to the gawkers.

At the movie ticket window, he unfolded then refolded his wallet to slide out his card and flicked it under the glass to the lady. He grabbed the pen in the tray, signed the receipt, put his copy in his wallet, and off we went, him opening all the doors for me as we went into the theater.

Later he took me on a driving tour of Birmingham giving me every detail of history, all the sports legends that came from there, the famous landmarks and city lights. At the gas station he smiled and said, "Do you want me to show off and pump the gas or are you satisfied?"

I smiled back. "I'm satisfied." And I got out and pumped the gas.

On my last night there, we watched the American Country Awards. I love the red carpet of award shows, but mostly I love critiquing the ladies in their dresses. Bob listened to my catty comments and laughed for a while. But soon, he was proactive.

"Okay, what's wrong with that one?"

I felt my uneasiness returning. My negativity was coming out again, this time about the beautiful women I'd never measure up to. I told Bob these ladies had the money and connections to look perfect so my expectations were high. He listened and nodded, but I became quiet.

I was focusing on the physical…and hyper-focused at that. It was all about the impression given by appearances, the pretense.

I glanced at him and the irony slammed into me like he slammed into doors.

A man with no arms or legs, scars all over his body, and not a negative word about anything or anyone. And me, an able-bodied woman so highly suspicious of his positive attitude and unending gratefulness for everything, criticizing beautiful women in sparkling gowns for not looking good enough. What must he have thought of me?

I'd been trained watching Joan and Melissa Rivers critique the red carpet, watching "educational" shows like "What Not To Wear" and noticing news anchors, sportscasters, and female reporters who are often drop-dead-gorgeous and mostly flawless. Something I secretly aspired to since childhood.

We all know the sensation of being around a person who lights up the room and makes you feel so good by bringing out the best in you. I had largely a similar experience being with Bob for those three days. Except that my worst was what came out; I hadn't realized there was so much of it. His gentle spirit, loving acceptance, and positive light shone bright against my darkness and long-held bitterness, and it all came tumbling out in unsavory remarks and attitudes that my great lipstick could not cover.

Bob's example forced me to stop and examine parts of myself I never wanted to show the light of day. Everyone who meets Bob is amazed at how he gets through life with such ease and independence. In the beginning, I was fixated on telling *that* story, explaining *how* he does what he does. It made me feel better about myself and all the advantages I enjoyed. It allowed me to ignore, for a time, the real story that was too shameful to accept.

I couldn't avoid the truth: here was a man who was doing life better than I was. By focusing on how he gets through life, I was completely missing out on who he really was.

I wasn't ready to receive it because I couldn't face who *I* was. In his speech at St. Mary's College I'd wanted to hear how he gets through a life of limitations hoping to find inspiration in how I could get through my own limitations. But there's the rub: *Bob doesn't see limitations.* He rejects them. He does everything he wants to do because what we call limitations he calls reality, and he doesn't complain about what he can't do because he's living life *on his own terms.*

He doesn't feel sorry for himself or feel that he's playing with a handicap. He doesn't have time to think about those things because he's giving everything he has.

The first draft was one thank you after another to everyone in his life. It was touching, but it wasn't answering my questions. He kept repeating that he was grateful for his childhood, that it was the best he could ever ask for, that the abuse and rejection was necessary because it made him tough to handle school, live life on his own, compete at the international level of quad rugby, etc. etc.

Necessary? I couldn't understand this acceptance and forgiveness. I thought he was glossing over the pain, stuffing it down. Why wasn't he angry? Why didn't he regret all that stuff in his childhood? His physical scars are obvious but what about the emotional scars? He had to be in denial or at least living a lie in some way.

But as I grilled him with questions that weekend and kept focused on how he lived, I began to sense how frustrated he must have been with me and how my questions always bent toward the negative and were often downright rude.

"Have you ever regretted your decision to live in light of all you've had to deal with? Have you ever contemplated suicide?"

No answer. He didn't want to go there. But I did. I thought for sure he was hiding something.

That was really why I'd visited.

How could he be okay? For some reason, as difficult as it is to admit, that was unthinkable to me.

I had travelled to Birmingham to get the *real* story. And, indeed; I did get the real story. I did find exactly what I was looking for: anger, bitterness, resentment, shame, fear. It was all there, my past seeping like puss into my present. My emotional wounds were like tumors on my soul. I hadn't healed the way Bob had. I was still playing the victim believing I wasn't good enough for anything or anyone. My physical presentation became my shield.

But my story in light of Bob's seemed ridiculous at best. As I fastened my seatbelt for the plane ride home, I was not only embarrassed by my attitude, but that I had walked around for so many years living as though I had wounds that were un-healable.

The truth of this gentle spirit with no arms or legs was so far out of my reach, I couldn't accept what was right in front of me.

Irving, Texas, age 6

The summer before his illness, his Little League Baseball team in NEWTON, KANSAS. BOBBY IS PICTURED IN CENTER TOP ROW. COUSIN PAUL GARIBAY is pictured on bottom row last on right, looking at picture.

Newton, Kansas, 1978, age 9

Top: Johnny, me, Lisa. Bottom: Paul and Willie. This is the group of cousins that skated together the night I got sick.

The Starlite Skating Rink where my cousins and I skated for the last time on January 6, 1979.

Dr. & Mrs. Rennebohm and Uncle Richard. I am so grateful for them.

We played games during his visit to my grandparents' house.

These two pictures were taken at my 10th birthday party and published in The Newton Kansan newspaper, July 16, 1979. We played baseball, darts, and hot potato. That's my dad in the background.

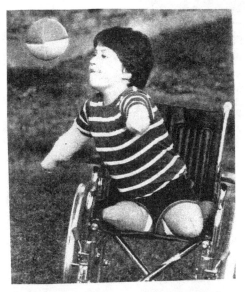

I played as much ball as I could that summer before leaving for an 8 month stay at the Chicago Rehabilitation Institute. Picture taken 1979 and published in the National Enquirer Dec. 2, 1980.

Tony Hill, wide receiver for the Dallas Cowboys, came to visit me in the hospital. He brought me this jacket and shirt!

DELIGHTED Bobby Lujano — who has no arms or legs — with some of the mail and gifts he received from over 4,000 Enquirer readers around the world.

Me showing that I could still perform the Eucharist before it was suggested I stop. The National Enquirer Dec 2, 1980.

Published in the National Enquirer February 24, 1979.

Pope John Paul II blessing me in Chicago on October 4, 1979. Officer Jim Zwitt is on the left. Vatican photo.

*Elda Bachman teaching me in my
Grandparents' basement. Lisa, Paul and
Willie liked to see what we were up to.*

*Me and Grandma Hope
showing off my first pair of
legs in the summer of 1980.*

*This was a fun night of dancing
at a high school dance!*

*High school
graduation, 1988.*

*Beginning my bachelor degree at the
University of Dallas as reported by the
Dallas Morning News, September, 1988.*

*These pictures depict my graduate studies from the
University of Tennessee as reported in March and
August of 1995 by The Knoxville News-Sentinel.*

The rivalry between Team Canada and USA continues. Joe Soares is in the middle pointing. Photo courtesy of TH!NKFilm from the documentary Murderball.

The seeds to my dreams and future in murderball were planted in Atlanta during the Paralympics.

I love that quad rugby is a full-contact sport but it's best to stay in your chair! Playing for the Lakeshore Demolition.

The Tree of Life at the opening ceremonies of the 2004 Paralympics in Athens, Greece. Photo Courtesy of Getty Images.

Bronze medal winners, 2004 Paralympics, Athens, Greece.

Playing for Team USA!

The Olympic and Paralympic athletes at the White House with President and Mrs. Bush after the games.

Team USA, 2004

Our interview on the Larry King Live show in 2005. From left: Scott Hogsett, Larry King, me, Keith Cavill, Andy Cohn, and Mark Zupan. Picture credit http://masdeporte.as.com

The marquee in Newton, Kansas, premiering the documentary Murderball.

*Two of our coaches,
James Gumbert
and Kevin Orr.*

*Me and my dad in Athens, Greece
after the bronze medal game.*

Me and Grandma Hope.

From left: Paul Garibay, Aunt Mary (Garibay), Will Jr., Uncle Gonzalo Navarro, Willie Garibay, sister Lisa, nephew Josh Oliver, Little Mary and Isaiah Garibay, brother Julian Lujano, Dad, (step)Mom Edna, brother Joe Lujano, John Lujano and Carol Lujano.

I can type 35 words per minute.

Me and Tara during her 3 day visit.

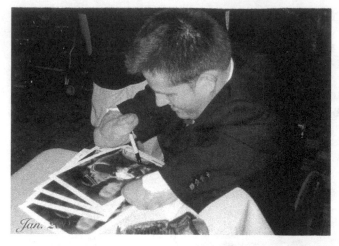

Signing autographs the night Tara and her family and I met at St. Mary's College in January of 2007.

Eating pizza with my elbows.

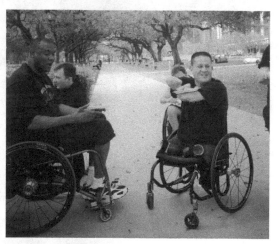

Instilling important lessons about health, fitness, and independence. This is what I love about my job.

At the White House Summit with NCHPAD staff and Paralympians in 2014. Commit to inclusion.

Quad Rugby, aka Murderball, is an amazing sport.

The day I stop wanting to be coached is the day I will stop playing.

"Being confident of this, that he who began a good work in you will carry it on to completion until the day of Christ Jesus."

Philippians 1:6 NIV

11

Leaving Home

I WAS STILL USING PROSTHETIC ARMS and legs when I learned to drive in the summer of 1988, right after high school graduation. I had taken the handicap bus (as it was called back then) to and from high school the last four years, but to get to college, I needed my own transportation. My first vehicle was a 2-door GMC Jimmy. The Jimmy had been fitted with hand controls that connected to the gas and brake pedals; the stems came up under the steering wheel.

The first time I took my dad for a ride after I received my license was a near disaster. It was 4:30 in the afternoon and as I drove down a residential street, a kid darted out from the sidewalk into my path. I slammed on the brakes and my dad cursed vehemently. I managed to avoid hitting the child and I proved to my dad, and to myself, that I had quick enough reflexes to handle the pressure of driving. Thank God. What an interesting moment.

I commuted to the University of Texas, Dallas, for eighteen months and then transferred to the University of Texas, Arlington. With the transfer of schools, it was time to transfer living spaces. I felt I had done everything I had to do to be a subordinate son. Now it was time to get out and be on my own. I was twenty-one years old and wanted to be my own man. In August of 1990, I drove my GMC Jimmy to the next city over, fifteen minutes away from home, and started the journey to become my own person.

I approached a guy named Jeff about being roommates. I had

111

known him for a handful of years but never really hung out with him. We had a mutual friend, we saw each other in church at St. Matthews where he was in the choir and performed in the band. He worked at UT Arlington as a computer operator. Jeff was friendly and very kind. He was eclectic, well-rounded, and traveled a lot, but the real clincher was that he would only charge $25 per week with free utilities. This was a positive situation in my estimation. He seemed the perfect choice.

Dad was scared. I believe he thought I'd never leave home so when I did, he was a bit surprised even though this was what we had been wanting and preparing for. My dad had Jeff investigated via a criminal background check! I told Jeff and he said, "I should be investigating you since you're moving into *my* house!" It was just Dad being Dad and Jeff was okay with him wanting to protect me.

Jeff was a great guy and I cherish the friendship we had. He taught me how to sing. We used to sit up late into the night and sing songs while he played guitar. I'm not a great singer but he showed me how to hold notes and read music. Our voices blended into the darkness until our eyes were too heavy to focus. I owe a lot to him for opening up his home to me. He was very caring and accepting. I am very thankful and appreciative of that early start toward independence.

I enjoyed taking care of myself, going to school, cleaning my room, doing laundry; it was all great but it was also short-lived. That September, I crashed my truck. Technically, my driver's license requires me to drive with my prosthetic arms, but I had learned to drive without them. I became much more comfortable behind the wheel driving with my elbows. Sometimes the bands on the prosthetic arms would break, rendering them unreliable at inopportune times, like right in the middle of traffic, so I taught myself to drive without them.

It was a Sunday and I was glued to the TV watching the Cowboys and the Giants. Jimmy Johnson was in his second year of coaching the Cowboys and they were 1-15. It was too early in the season and his career to know that this second season would be the beginning of his reign of glory. All I knew at the time was at halftime, the Cowboys were losing 14-7, and the phone was ringing.

"Can you give me a ride down to the stadium?" It was my friend Sonia. "We're selling cookies in the booth for the soccer team and my shift starts at 1:30."

Annoyed, I figured that if I hurried, I could be back before missing too much of the third quarter. I picked her up at church and we headed off on the freeway toward the stadium. The gas lever moved easily under the direction of my elbow, pushing to ten miles above the speed limit. The wind was hot coming through the open windows, blowing Sonia's hair and making me sweat.

Suddenly, out of nowhere, one of the tires blew out. The steering wheel tightened and the Jimmy started to shake. I couldn't control it. We went from the fast lane to the middle lane, the brake was jammed. I yelled for Sonia to grab the brake lever but it was stuck. We clipped the back of a van in front of us and flipped over.

I'd blacked out. Sonia later said that we flew out of the truck after the first flip. We both ejected out the passenger window, and the truck continued to flip five or six more times. I woke up on the sidewalk looking into a man's face. His red hair was neatly in place.

"Can you move?" His blue eyes were anxious.

"Yes." I could feel every painful limb.

"Do you know your name?"

"Bob Lujano."

"Do you know where you are, Bob?"

I hesitated. "On the side of the road?"

He rolled his eyes.

Ambulance sirens blew in the distance; this wasn't good. I asked for Sonia. She sat on the sidewalk a few feet from where I'd landed like a sack of potatoes, with only a few bruises and scrapes. Thank God. The wail of the sirens got louder and louder. The rescue was for me. There was blood everywhere. The paramedics loaded my crumpled body onto a gurney and into the ambulance. In the emergency room, the staff worked quickly but didn't seem overly anxious so I guessed I wasn't going to die.

"Who's winning the game?" I asked. They didn't answer.

I wasn't aware of my injuries but I knew I didn't feel good. The nurses began asking me a lot of questions and prepped me for immediate surgery. I was impressed with their quick decisions and methodical movements. The short bone in my left leg was broken and piercing through the skin and my right shoulder was separated. I had a fracture in my left hip and my face looked like I'd been in the ring with Mike Tyson. My twice-amputated leg would be shortened for a third time. As the staff hustled around me, a police officer stood in the corner, staring at me. The poor guy didn't look happy. He slowly walked up to me, blinked a few times and leaned over to whisper in my ear.

"I'm so sorry, sir, but I couldn't find your arms or legs."

I wanted to laugh out loud! The poor guy must have been frantic at the crash site wondering where all my limbs had disappeared to.

"It's okay, sir. You're not going to find them," I said. "I don't have any." I tried to smile and winced at the pain.

"You mean you were driving with no arms or legs?"

The look in his eyes was so comical. It makes me laugh to this day. His face contorted and I could see him trying to wrap his mind around this, to get the visual, but it wasn't happening. He quickly switched gears and his eyes narrowed.

"Do you have car insurance?"

"Yes, sir, I do. The proof of insurance card is in the truck."

He cited me on the spot for no insurance since I couldn't produce it! He also cited me for driving with my elbows. I guess he wasn't as amused as I was. The nurses did their final prep for surgery and whisked me down the hall. So much for a Sunday afternoon of football.

The Cowboys lost 28-7.

With my new injuries and no mode of transportation, I had to move back home so my Dad and step-mom could take care of me. After my brief taste of independence before the accident, I was now more resolved than ever to make this stay a short one. I'm grateful to them for taking care of me during those months, but at the time it was a giant "note-to-self": a dependent lifestyle was not what I wanted. The accident scared my family. It brought back terrible memories for them from the past. They were afraid maybe I wasn't ready or capable to be on my own after all. I saw the worry and concern in their faces and I did not like what I saw. I also didn't like how it made me feel like a little kid again. Needing constant help, or having a 24-hour caretaker, was not how I was going to do life. So I hammered on the physical therapy, which was old hat by now, and made plans to leave.

The goal for rehab was different this time. Previously, I needed to learn to walk on the prosthetic legs, which carried me from middle school to my first days in college. This time, I was actually losing my legs for good. My left leg had been longer than my right, which allowed me to balance and lean on it as I walked with the crutch on the right side. But now that it was amputated again because of the accident, it was too short to balance on. I tried walking with the legs several times but kept falling over. I couldn't stand up properly or walk a straight line. I was a drunken sailor without the drink!

This was slightly disappointing but it didn't matter. I had my chair, I could still drive, and I could still take care of myself. I didn't need legs to get through school. As long as I had wheels I was good to go.

A mere four months later, in January of 1991, I was back on track and packing my bags. I was also driving a new GMC Blazer, thanks to the insurance money. Jeff was gracious to keep the room for me in his house in Arlington and we quickly got back to our friendship. I loved the lightheartedness that came with being on my own. No guilt, no subordination, just pure jovial freedom like a regular guy.

Jeopardy became our favorite show. In the evenings, after class and homework, we watched a recorded version and battled wits. We were great competitors, but Jeff was better than me. I always won the sports and history questions and he always won the literature and music. We both loved this nightly ritual. Jeff also taught me the importance of novels and to develop a taste for the eclectic. He played guitar, wrote music, and developed in me an appreciation for acoustic songs, folk music, and Christian music.

I went to mass every Sunday and studied hard at UT Arlington. In addition to Jeff, a new group of friends on campus made for a great experience. The highlight was wheelchair basketball. I wasn't a great player but I made it through the tryouts to earn a spot on the team. I enjoyed the workouts and bonding with the other players. This was a wonderful community for me to be in. We went on to win collegiate championships and a few of the players went pro. One guy got me a wheelchair specifically for basketball. I will always be grateful for that. The environment at UT was great because they have many facilities and systems for the disabled and there were many disabled people on campus. All-in-all I had a typical college experience.

Interesting how living on your own, the entire decision-making process is now yours to enjoy or exploit. No more fear of retribution from Dad. I was free.

One day my good friend from high school, Bobby Haines, came over and said there was a gentlemen's club down the street we needed to go check out. I agreed. I definitely enjoyed what was going on inside those walls. The next day, Bobby came back to my house.

"Let's go to Sensations," he says.

"We just went yesterday," I say.

"Yeah, let's go again!" he says.

All of the sudden, it had been a month that we'd gone to this place every Friday, Saturday and Sunday. I began to question myself: I've seen it and enjoyed it; now what? Do I want one of them to be my girlfriend? I ran into a girl from high school one night. I knew her family. The mind games were getting to be too much. I didn't want to go anymore. I wasted money and emotions thinking I would actually be involved with one of the dancing girls. I decided I was done. I didn't care to make this a longer habit. It wasn't my cup of tea.

Bobby wanted to keep going and he gave me a hard time at first when I said I was done. But eventually we started doing other things like cruising and trying to meet girls legitimately. I wanted relationships that were real. I wanted to meet college girls who did other things.

I was very fortunate to have Bobby and Jeff in my life while I was learning to live on my own and deciding what kind of a man I wanted to be. I enjoyed being independent and the responsibilities that came with it. I liked learning from my own decisions. I knew I wanted to make something of my life. I wanted to be proud of myself. I studied hard, played hard, exercised hard, dated girls (though they still weren't taking me seriously), and in 1993 I earned my Bachelor of Arts in History and Pre-Law. I am so thankful for that milestone.

When I graduated from UT Arlington, I either wanted to study law or follow my love for sports so I sent applications to two schools to see which one would stick. I applied to law school at Stanford and graduate school at UT Knoxville for a degree in Sports Management. My application was turned down by Stanford, and I was one of three students being considered for the last spot at Tennessee. I saw this as the Lord confirming my path. I had to go through an interview process before being accepted into the program. My dad and I met with Dr. Gene Hayes, and it was the fifth grade all over again.

"There are three people vying for this last opening. It's a strict program," he said, soaking in my appearance.

"Don't be blinded by his physical limitations. Don't close the door of opportunity on him," said my dad.

"If I give him the seat in the program, he can't turn in anything less than a 'B' or he's out," said Dr. Hayes.

"He can do that," said my dad.

"I want to hear it from Bob," said Dr. Hayes.

"Yes, I can do it. I would really like to be a part of this program," I said. Luckily I had good grades in my undergraduate work to back me up.

I called my dad a few days later to tell him the good news. I was accepted! The Texas Department of Human Services would again pay my tuition. Strangely enough, my dad had transferred with Phillips Company from Dallas to Knoxville. Typically, graduate students did not live on campus so I asked if I could stay with him. He said sure! He was thrilled. I did not see this move as a regression back to dependence. In my mind this was only a short-term arrangement to complete my masters and then I would be on my way. A graduate degree in Sports Management, my passion, was a giant step toward independence so I did not hesitate to move back home with my dad, step-mom, and two stepbrothers to commute to school.

The Knoxville area is beautiful amid the Smokey Mountain backdrop. I was very fortunate to attend a school with a big college atmosphere. This was my first experience at a major university. At UT Arlington I was exposed to wheelchair sports and a big community of disabled athletes but it didn't compare to the big college experience in Knoxville. Football Saturdays were always fun because the team ranked in the top ten of its league and won many of their games. It would soon be the alma mater to Peyton Manning. I was very fortunate to be a part of the Tennessee Wheelbillies basketball team. I still wasn't a great player but I had speed and could hit lay-ups. We grew to a big competitive team. We didn't win any championships but we had fun and it was great to be a student athlete and bond with a new community.

I fell in love with one of the standout able-bodied basketball players there, Nikki McCray. She was beautiful, smart, and talented with a great record. I loved watching her play. Both working on sports degrees, we shared a class together and had a great friendship. Her smile was bright and warm and lit up the room, and my soul. Her laugh was contagious, her spirit a magnet. We studied a few times, talked sports, and I watched her dunk ball after ball during the games. If it was up to me, we would have gotten married. But her future was not with me.

One of the requirements to earn my master's degree was to complete an internship. Dr. Jack Parsley, a member of the faculty, approached me one spring day on campus and asked what my plans were. I knew immediately; the Olympic and Paralympic Games were coming to Atlanta, Georgia in 1996. The disabled community is every bit as athletic as the able-bodied and I wanted to be as close as I could get to the elite athletes of the world.

"I'm interested in going to Atlanta to work with the Paralympic Games," I said.

"Let me get a hold of my friend Max. He's the current Secretary of State for Georgia. I contribute to his campaign fund. I would be happy to setup an appointment between the two of you. I'm sure he has contacts. Can you drive to Atlanta to meet with him?"

"Of course!" I replied with a huge smile. I knew this was divine intervention.

I drove three hours to the state capital building, so excited. The golden dome atop the building glistened in the sun, marking my target as I drove through the streets of downtown Atlanta. Inside, the floors were covered in marble. Antique styled oak paneling covered the walls, marble busts, flags of every kind and pictures hung from every wall.

Secretary of State Cleland greeted me warmly and promptly rolled out the red carpet. I felt like royalty in this grand place. We went into his office and he began telling me about his status as a triple amputee. He was a captain in Viet Nam. He and two other soldiers had just been dropped off by a Helicopter and were watching it take off when he noticed a grenade lying on the ground. The pin wasn't properly fastened and as he reached for it, it exploded, taking his legs and arm. Captain Cleland later discovered the grenade had belonged to one of the other soldiers who had climbed out of the helicopter just moments before. It fell off his flak jacket.

He published a book about it called, *Strong at the Broken Places*. It was sitting on his shelf. I knew that story, even though I had not read the book. I didn't need to. I was familiar with being broken, having to take on a new identity as a quadruple amputee, and being strong anyway. I pondered his words, and his missing limbs.

"What can I do for you, Bob?" Flat out, no beating around the bush; he was here to help me.

"I would really like to work for the Paralympic Games, Mr. Cleland," I said, shifting in my chair.

"Please, call me Max," he said.

I'm not sure why, but I felt flush.

"A friend of mine is involved with the Paralympics. I will give him a call and see if we can't get you in somewhere. Do you have a resume'?"

"Yes I do," I said, pulling it out of my bag and handing it to him.

And as quick as I could snap my finger, if I had one, it was done. He made several phone calls and two weeks later I received my own phone call of acceptance. I will always be grateful to him. Just like that, I was on my way to the next phase in my life.

I didn't know it then, but the pieces to my dreams were about to come together. I didn't know that Atlanta was the piece that would bring back a part of me lost at the age of nine, cut off and disposed of along with my four limbs. As far as I knew, I was just going to the Paralympics to complete my internship. But in reality, I was about to experience life to the fullest. My convictions would soon be tested beyond measure. Soon, opportunities I thought were lost would be rediscovered. I'd find excitement beyond my wildest hopes and fantasies and would embark on a journey that would bring me ultimate fulfillment. Many things I thought impossible, I would do.

But at that time, I simply packed my bags, leaving home for the third and final time, and headed to Atlanta to find a place to live.

"It happens so regularly that it's predictable. The moment I decide to do good, sin is there to trip me up. I truly delight in God's commands, but it's pretty obvious that not all of me joins in that delight. Parts of me covertly rebel, and just when I least expect, they take charge. I've tried everything and nothing helps. I'm at the end of my rope. Is there no one who can do anything for me? Isn't that the real question? The answer, thank God, is that Jesus Christ can and does. He cared to set things right in this life of contradictions where I want to serve God with all my heart and mind, but am pulled by the influence of sin to do something totally different."

Romans 7:21-25 MSG

12

The Rolling Twenties

MY FIRST DAY THERE, I thought I would get the best hotel I could find, considering I'd be living there for three to four months. I wanted to be comfortable. However, my paid internship as Assistant Director of Accreditation for the swim trials didn't afford me many choices for a roof over my head. I found a hotel off 10th Street that was close to work, but I soon discovered it wasn't a safe area. I regularly heard sirens and gun shots.

Once, about two or three in the morning, there was a knock on my door. A shiver went up my spine. I thought I was in danger, that I was about to be robbed or murdered, or both. I didn't answer. I just lay there in the dark, sweating and trying not to breathe too loudly. I couldn't do anything about my racing heart but I wished it would be quiet. My body pushed into the mattress. After a long minute, heavy shoes took the person away from my door, thank God. I didn't like being afraid, but sometimes there are circumstances we all have to put up with, just things we have to endure.

During the last month of my internship, the Olympic Committee signed an agreement for housing in the brand new dorms at Georgia Tech for the Paralympic workers. What a difference to be in a brand new room on a college campus. I really enjoyed those four weeks of peace and safety.

I was hired as a full-time employee of the Paralympic Games right out of the internship. I went back to the University of Tennessee for my formal graduation ceremony, with a Master of Science in Sports Management, and then started in September of 1995 as a Venue Director for the City Hall East project for the Paralympic Games. Out of necessity, my venue was the first to be operational since I would be handling all the volunteers for the games.

I worked at APOC East, where I was in charge of training, accrediting, and dispensing uniforms for 12,000 volunteers! We put press releases out to the public to ask for volunteers to work at the games. I think the whole city of Atlanta showed up! There were so many people trying to fill out applications that the building managers threatened to shut down the entire building because we were way over capacity for the fire codes. However, we were in the City Hall East building and they didn't want to shut the whole thing down, so I had to kick everyone out of my area to avoid shutting down the city offices in the other part of the building. It was a big crisis, but I handled it and got everyone out. I didn't want the CEO of the games to get mad and fire me right off the bat.

How appropriate that a disabled person would head up the volunteer accreditation department. I knew firsthand how I wanted to be treated as a disabled person so it was a no-brainer to train the volunteers. I wrote policy and procedure manuals, worked with the city coordinators, and even coordinated structure changes to the building. There I was, working at the second biggest sporting event in the world, at one of the largest venues in the games, being paid well, in a city with great nightlife and home to the Braves, the World Series champions in '95. Secretary Cleland sent me football tickets to the Georgia Dome. I was in heaven as I watched the Cowboys beat the Falcons, 28-13. This was a glorious day and a glorious season of my life. What could be better?

It was also an important step in my relationship with my dad. He had not been emotional in front of me very many times but he broke down when he came and saw my office and all the responsibilities I had. It was my first job, right out of graduate school. He would tell me years later that when he saw me at work, negotiating with the Mayor of the city, looking for building space, and seeing the boxes and boxes of uniforms, enough for 12,000 volunteers, clothing them, training them, accrediting them…it was the first time he exhaled since my amputations. He could see I was in an important position. I was going to make it and I'd be okay in the world and be able to provide for myself. This was the moment of truth for him. He kept telling me how proud he was of me—first driving a car, then getting my masters, and now my very first job at a worldwide sporting event.

The city of Atlanta was the place to be in 1995 and 1996. It was like the roaring twenties. The city was alive with festivities and parties, both from the World Series and in anticipation of the Olympic Games. I was quite taken with the glamorous atmosphere. It was common to see celebrities and sports figures walking down the sidewalk: Evander Holyfield, Tom Glavine, Andre Risen, and wrestler Dallas Diamond Page were only a few.

The 1996 Atlanta Paralympics were also the first to attract worldwide corporate sponsorship. This meant more people in the city, more perks, and more excitement. When we wore our credentials in the city, we were invited to special places where movie stars hung out. We saw Arnold Schwarzenegger, Bruce Willis and Demi Moore. Restaurants offered us free food and the bars gave us free drinks. It was a once in a lifetime experience.

During the year-long preparation for the games, I desperately wanted to play a part of the sports scene after work. I had enjoyed playing basketball. There was a team at the Shepherd Center Hospital and Recreation Facility that I joined but I was once again relegated to the bench. Wheelchair basketball is better suited for paraplegics with long arms. Sensing my frustration, Bill Furbish, who worked in the technology department for the Games, introduced me to another sport being played at the Shepherd Center. His simple question would change my life forever.

"Have you ever heard of murderball? Quad rugby?" he asked.

"I heard of it during my time at UTA, but I've never seen it played. Why?"

"You need to come with me to see it in action. I think you'd be good at it," he said with a smile.

I wasn't sure but I agreed to meet him at the Shepherd Center. When I got there, I couldn't believe my eyes. I watched a whole team of quadriplegic men, sitting in gladiator-type chairs, rolling around a basketball court trying to get the ball over the opposing line to score a goal. They slammed into each other on purpose with their heavy duty chairs. Each time it sounded like a car crash. It was a cross between rugby, football and basketball—full-contact, and it actually made me giddy watching them! I was floored by their speed and quick-turning chairs.

As we sat on the sidelines, Bill explained. "Quad rugby was invented by the Canadians and originally called Murderball. It was specifically developed for athletes who are quadriplegics, usually from spinal injury on the C4 or lower vertebrae. Because the injury is lower, they have partial mobility in the arms and legs allowing them to be independent. Christopher Reeve's injury was at C1-C2, rendering him with no mobility below the neck. However, anyone who has functional impairment in all four limbs can play; it's not just for those with spinal injuries," said Bill.

A shout went up. *Score!* The teammates high-fived each other.

"The Canadians also developed player classifications," Bill continued, "to take into consideration the varying degrees of mobility. Each player on the team is given a classification number based on medical tests. There are 7 levels of classification: .5, 1.0, 1.5, 2.0, 2.5, 3.0, and 3.5. The classification numbers of each player on the court at any given time are added together and the maximum point value allowed on the court per team is 8.0. This allows everyone to play by keeping the teams even in skill."

Two of the players bashed into each other and one of them fell over and landed on his face. He lay there upside down until the referees came over to upright him and his chair by putting a piece of cardboard on the floor and under his wheel and then yanking him up.

Bill smiled. "It's played in four 8-minute periods for 32 minutes. In real time, it takes about an hour and 15 to complete a game. We slam into each other on purpose while trying to pass, dribble, and carry the ball into the goal box on a regulation size basketball court. A team has ten seconds to inbound the ball and fifteen seconds to cross mid-court while trying to bounce the ball once every ten seconds or pass it to a teammate. Once the team is on the other side of the court, the object is to score a point by taking possession and crossing two wheels over the goal line."

I couldn't wipe the smile from my face. Bill sat in his day chair and pushed his rugby chair towards me.

"Get in," he said, matching my smile with his own.

I hopped in his chair and felt the aluminum wheels beneath me. They were at a funny angle.

"Lessens the damage from impact," he said, soaking in my excitement.

He got the attention of the coach and sat on the sidelines as I took my place on the court with the other players. A guy tossed me the ball. I caught it with ease and passed it to another player. I discovered I still had good ball-handling; I was still Shooter even with just my elbows. I could catch the ball and then put it in my lap and wheel down the court at a high rate of speed.

I was home! I had found my sport!

I joined the Atlanta Rolling Thunder without hesitation. For a while, I played quad rugby on Mondays and Wednesdays, wheelchair basketball on Tuesdays and Thursdays, and I swam on Fridays. But I knew right away that quad rugby was the right fit. For a long time when I smashed into the other players, I did it with a smile on my face. There was a deep satisfaction I hadn't felt in a long, long time.

The veteran players were up in age and moving on which was fortunate timing for me. They were looking for new, young players. Bill Furbish was my first rugby mentor. He knew all about being an elite athlete. He medaled in track for the 1988 Paralympics in Seoul, South Korea. The first thing Bill taught me was the rules and nuances of the game. Bill also gave me my first rugby chair. It was a real clunker but you don't want a new one until you're in it for the long haul. New chairs are $3000. But like a first car, if you take care of it, the new car will not be far behind. The loaner was just fine.

Bill saw I had speed and quickness. My main strength was being able to move laterally. In the wheelchair world this is known as side to side. However, Bill was quick to point out that no matter how fast I was, it would be no good if I couldn't catch and throw the ball. These simple but profound words stayed with me as a new player. I had to prove myself many times that I could handle throwing and catching. I was classified as a 2.0 player because according to the rules "I cannot hold or grip the ball with my hands or fingers" but I have good shoulder strength.

My biggest problem on the court was staying in my chair. Being a quad amputee, I am unlike the majority of quads who are paralyzed. They at least have legs to strap to a wheelchair to hold them still. I did not. Whenever I was hit, I'd go lunging or sprawling forward and out of my chair. Being knocked out of my chair brought me a lot of ribbing.

"You look like Rocky the flying squirrel!" one of my teammates guffawed.

Oh my. This was bad. I'd sometimes land on top of another player too, which resulted in a penalty against me. If I had possession and was knocked out, it would result in a turnover and the other team would get possession.

Eventually this became the strategy of every team that played against the Rolling Thunder from '95-'98. It was effective, and at the very least, it was good entertainment for the fans.

So here I was, in the sport I felt destined to play and right away I was the new comedy act. They did not view me as a serious player. But it led me to look for many creative ways to keep myself strapped in. I couldn't find a solution that worked very well so it was an ongoing problem.

Still, the Rolling Thunder enjoyed success in the United States Quadriplegic Rugby Association (USQRA). Most local club teams are members of this association. With teammates like Bill Furbish, Bert Burns, Kurt Bonyell, Mark Zupan and the coaching of Wendy Gumbert, we eventually placed in the top five at the national level. I had quick success in my first few years, attended many rugby tournaments and was becoming a solid player. Ironically, it was the worst thing that could have happened because my play was being noticed. I was winning all-tournament awards like "Best Class 2.0" and the highly coveted "Sportsmanship Award," which is not really coveted.

Winning all-tournament awards was like a popularity contest or the flavor-of-the-month club. Winning the Sportsmanship award was like, "let's hear it for the most disabled person who tried the hardest." *Yeah Bob!* I didn't see the reality of it yet though, so to me it was, "You're a great man, Bob! You might as well throw your name into the Heisman trophy race."

At that time, as strange as it sounds, I thought I was "God's gift" to rugby. I thought I was going to save the Rolling Thunder. My ego was really high. I would always be 12th on the basketball team but in rugby, I could throw the special-made chair all over the place. I was good at passing, I could fly down the court, I could do everything the game required. I was seeing fireworks. This was it.

My dream of being a professional baseball or football player had been tossed aside with my diseased limbs, but now, with quad rugby, I had a chance to be a top-level athlete. My dream was back. It looked different than what I had imagined, but I didn't care. For the first time since my amputations I had found a sport I could go all out with. I egged on the opposing players to bash into me. I wanted to be the best. I wanted to be in their face. All those years of pent-up energy thinking my ball playing days were over was releasing with a vengeance. I had some catching up to do.

Fortunately, the second thing Bill taught me was rebalancing with humility. In hindsight, I knew I wasn't "all that." Not even close. I was a babe in the woods with much to learn and accomplish and Bill wasn't going to let me miss this lesson. He put my false ego in check and I am so grateful to him for setting me straight. I had to learn to listen to the coach and do what he asked. I had to learn not to talk back. I had to learn to be a part of the team. My father's words came back to me, thank goodness. I had to know my place and respect the authority in front of me. It was a hard lesson, but necessary.

After work and rugby practices my friend Jim and I hit the town, my newly-found physical high spurring us on. And when our other friend Jay joined us, we were three wild and crazy guys! We frequented a crowded sports bar called the 3 Dollar Café to eat wings and watch Braves games and later, the Tyson-Holyfield fights. Then we would push over to the Chilly Pepper and Pat Hurley's to go dancing. The place was always packed. Hip Hop and a mix of dance music blared out the door and into the street. Jim and I liked to go to places to meet women of ethnic backgrounds. Nothing against white women, but "Hotlanta" was a place you could meet various women of different cultures: Asian, Latin, Middle Eastern. It was intoxicating. The lights swirled around us as we danced, watching the throng of bodies dance around us.

Jim was a magnet for beautiful women. Sometimes he approached them and sometimes they approached him. Either way, I was a beneficiary to the company and conversation. They would talk for an hour or so and then he would ask them, "Who do you trust more? Jim or Bob?" They would always say Bob! Jim was mischievous with a great personality. It was good for me to hang around him, to be afforded the many possibilities for meeting beautiful women and the fun that he brought. We stayed out late. Jim and Jay always seemed to push the limit of fun and excess. I was just along for the ride. I do remember having my limits and knowing when to come home, but not always.

As a team member of the Atlanta Rolling Thunder and a full-time worker for the Paralympic Games, we were treated like Kings by the city of Atlanta. Bona fide royalty, we were. There was always someone wanting to meet us or buy us drinks. I felt like the toast of the town. I watched the professional athletes walk down the street in downtown and paid attention to how they reacted with the fans. I found myself falling into a culture I wasn't aware of. A lifestyle that seemed like something I wanted but didn't realize the consequences. The city was on fire with sports. Free drinks, free food, come eat here, all because we played wheelchair sports and worked for the Para's. The city catered to us and we accepted. Every Friday and Saturday night the city was jumping with excitement, dancing, partying till all hours. We went to clubs and asked girls to dance, twenty-five at a time. It was so easy to get caught up in the euphoria. Watching the professionals, I thought this was okay. This was the lifestyle an athlete was supposed to lead.

I didn't totally forget all my values but I was on my own and making my own decisions, good and bad. I had two degrees under my belt, I was out of my dad's house, I was an independent adult living in one of the largest cities in the nation, and like the prodigal son I fell off the wagon for a while. I had many late nights of partying. I couldn't see myself. I didn't recognize I had gotten caught up in something that wasn't really me. Much of this was due to the wheelchair rugby. Similar to the able-bodied rugby in that you go out after games to the bars and meet the ladies and get drunk. I didn't get as far as drunk, but I liked going out and partying and meeting the women. I was still waiting to meet the girl of my dreams and have a real relationship, so I got caught up in the lifestyle just like anyone. Work hard, practice hard, and then party hard; that was how it was.

I spent my birthday at the now bankrupt and infamous Gold Club, a so-called "gentleman's" club; ironic because I don't remember acting like a gentleman. We sat in the VIP section and whooped it up with the working ladies. I was, quite literally, not in Kansas anymore. It was pretty much a Studio 54 experience for me, except for the drug use; it never has and never will appeal to me. But I did enjoy the nightlife.

After almost a year of preparation, the time finally came for the 1996 Paralympic games to begin. Spectators for the games numbered around 300,000 and there were approximately 3,500 athletes from over 100 countries around the world. It felt like the whole world was in Atlanta. It was thrilling to have all my hard work come to fruition. On the night of the opening ceremony, my family and many friends were there in the stadium. I took pride in the fact that there were thousands of volunteers wandering around, all doing what they were supposed to. I had done my job.

As I watched the Paralympic torch being brought into the darkened stadium, hooked to a wheelchair, I thought it was magical and so pretty. A guy with no legs jumped out of an airplane and landed in the stadium. Christopher Reeve hosted the evening. He had only been a quadriplegic for one year. During his opening speech he said to the crowd of 64,000, "To be surrounded by people who believe in you is one of life's most precious gifts. Look around you and see how many people believe in you." The crowd went wild. His words are so true.

During the games, wheelchair rugby made its Paralympic debut as an exhibition sport. It was exciting to watch, especially since I was now on a team. The elite athletes were amazing and I salivated at the thought of being one of them. The American team won a ceremonial gold medal and we were euphoric.

I was thrilled with my first job at the Paralympics. I felt strongly that this is what I wanted to do as a career; I wanted to play, teach, and coach wheelchair sports. It was all a surreal experience. It's not every day that an entire city embraces you. It was like Disneyland. But it was short lived. I wanted to savor and soak it in. For two weeks I worked, watched the various events, and did not stop smiling.

The closing ceremony was a blast. I hung out and celebrated with many of the rugby guys. Willie Hernandez, the basketball player, showed up and somehow managed to sneak onto the field with the Puerto Rican team! That was funny. He's a nice guy. I also met Jerry Lee Lewis backstage that night. When I went up to shake hands with him, he looked at me and said in Southern drawl, "There really isn't much of you, is there boy?" I laughed hysterically. "No sir," I said. "No there's not."

After the close of the Paralympic Games, my friends and I and many other revelers wanted to keep the party going. I was still caught up in the party scene, hanging out with the boys, drinking one too many drinks, leading a decadent lifestyle, but I was discouraged because even though I had met many women in Atlanta, I still did not have a serious girlfriend. Many men in Atlanta were professionals, in addition to the athletes, trying to climb the corporate ladder. I was doubtful I could compete with them. We continued the late nights and the drinking, but most importantly, we kept the "babe radar" on high tilt.

It was then, a few months after the games had ended, that the elusive piece of the puzzle, the one I thought about only in my wildest dreams and fantasies, presented itself to me in the form of a beautiful woman named *Ruby.

"Is anyone crying for help? God is listening, ready to rescue you. If your heart is broken, you'll find God right there; if you're kicked in the gut, he'll help you catch your breath. Disciples so often get into trouble; still, God is there every time."

Psalm 34:17-19 MSG

13

The Ultimate Challenge in Life

J IM AND I AND A few other friends went to a place called The
Chamber. Smoke hung in the air barely visible in the darkened
lights. Marilyn Manson and Nine Inch Nails blared from an
unseen source. Most of the crowd was dressed in black, Gothic attire.
Ominous eyes peered out from behind black liner, white faces and
black lips. Black hair and multiple piercings were in vogue.

This dark and mysterious club was not a great place to dance or
meet women. Past experience told us that some of the attendees like
to hide or change their gender; asking a "woman" to dance was risky.
The music was not conducive to partnering-up on the dance floor.
We went for the shock value. It was really weird. This just wasn't
something that we saw walking around Atlanta every day.

It never occurred to me that I would meet anyone serious in such
a strange place. Quite frankly, it was beginning to occur to me that
I might not meet anyone serious in *any* of the clubs, let alone one as
dark as this. Maybe *I* was the freak show out there dancing on the
dance floor. Maybe *I* was viewed as the shock value figure. It isn't
too often you see a guy with no arms or legs. And dancing was as far
as anyone had wanted to go with me.

We were about to leave Gothic city when I noticed her; even
through the smoky haze her bright smile caught my eye. She was
beautiful. And sitting with another man. This should have been a
boundary issue, a red flag that I should have avoided; you don't move

in on someone else's girl even if she looks miserable. But at that point of my life, I was desperate for the one thing I never had. I just wanted female companionship, someone to love me back and take me seriously so we could live life together. I became blinded by my need to be validated beyond my limbs to the point of recklessness. Her beauty was intoxicating. There was no question about her gender; she was all female. I watched them for a while, wondering what their relationship might be. He didn't take her out on the dance floor. They just sat. So I moved in.

"Hi!" I yelled above the music. "Would you like to dance?"

Her companion sized me up, and then looked at her. He was a man of few words.

"Sure," she said without looking in his direction.

We went out on the floor and bounced around as best we could to the erratic, head-throbbing beat. The music seemed to go on forever as we moved back and forth. My friends pushed through the crowd as we came off the floor for a drink.

"There's nothing going on here, let's go," Jim screamed in my ear.

"What do you mean there's nothing going on?" I screamed back. "I just danced with a woman and she invited me to hang out at her table!"

I wasn't leaving just yet. I rolled away from Jim over to Ruby's table. We talked as best we could above the noise but I was a third wheel. Even though her date was silent, and seemed indifferent, it was awkward. It should have been an internal gut check, but it wasn't. I scribbled my name and number on a piece of paper and shoved it in her direction.

"Call me if you're ever available!" I shouted.

She leaned over and kissed me, right in front of the other guy; another red flag that I should have caught. I grinned and left with my friends. We went to a few other clubs and I was high on the kiss I had collected.

Two weeks went by and I hadn't thought much more about it until the phone rang.

"Hi. This is Ruby. Do you remember me from The Chamber a couple of weeks ago?"

"Sure I remember," I said. "I haven't kissed any girls since then!"
I laughed.

"Would you like to get together?" she asked.

"I would love to!" I said a little too enthusiastically, my voice
heading up an octave.

We lived about 35 miles apart so we agreed to meet in the middle.
She stepped out of her car and as she walked over to me, I noticed
she was as beautiful in the daylight as she was in the dark club. Her
African-American skin was smooth and radiant. Her eyes smiled,
matching the brightness I remembered. She was tall and confident
and walking straight towards *me*. We immediately embraced and
picked up the affection we parted with two weeks earlier. We sat
on the tailgate of my blazer kissing, hugging and having non-stop
conversation. I was euphoric. I invited her to my house that weekend
and the relationship sped into overdrive. Scars and all, limbs or
not, it didn't matter. I entered the part of the female world I had not
previously been invited to; a place I thought I might never experience.
I took her to dinner and late into the night, we made love.

Ruby loved me like there was no tomorrow. A flood of joy burst
out of me like the Hallelujah Chorus. This type of unconditional love
was what I had been waiting for all those years; my first serious
relationship had arrived and I thoroughly enjoyed every passionate
moment, many times over. In the early days we couldn't get enough
of each other. Despite the 35-mile distance between us and our busy
schedules, we somehow found ways to be together. I had years of
pent up energy to spend from the plethora of women who had not
wanted to take me for anything more than just a nice guy. I was still
a nice guy but now my severed body was being loved and validated
unconditionally. She caressed my brokenness, kissed my scars, and
loved my short limbs. I loved her back as best I could. I tried to
convey the gratefulness I felt in her complete acceptance of me. Deep
inside, it was the 4th of July fireworks, Christmas, and my birthday
all rolled into one. This was a gift I wanted to keep on opening.

She was 32; I was 25. Not quite *The Graduate*, but an older
woman nonetheless. Two weeks into the relationship we talked about
what the state of our affair was and where we were in our lives. She

was experienced; she had been married and divorced and was raising an eight year-old son. She was working for a telephone company as a supervisor. I was inexperienced and still partying. The games had come and gone and I hadn't landed in a career yet so I was bouncing from job to job to make ends meet. I had just started a new job selling urological supplies to quadriplegics with some of the guys on the Rolling Thunder. Ruby lived in the same city where my job was located. She suddenly threw her cards out on the table.

"Why don't you move in with me? We could split the cost of room and board and you would save a lot of gas money," she stated rather matter-of-factly.

I pondered her suggestion: Her apartment was three miles from my job. My apartment was 35 miles away. I would indeed save money. From a financial standpoint it made perfect sense.

I also pondered her suggestion with my heart. Was this the right thing to do? I was leery. I had only known her for a short time. I wanted her. I had waited many years for a woman to take me seriously. This woman was taking me seriously. She was offering to share her life with me.

Ruby was the first so I was naïve enough to think she must be "the one." I ignored all the red flags waving furiously in front of my face and convinced myself this was my chance to have a deep relationship. I had always wanted to get married. I had envisioned many times how a relationship before marriage would go. My relationship with Ruby started off unusual and currently didn't look like anything I had planned or dreamt about but I didn't let that dissuade me. Denial is powerful. There was a woman in front of me who wanted me in her bed so I decided this was the way to get married.

"You're right, it would be cost effective," I told her and hesitated. "When should we move my stuff?"

I was in way over my head. I woke up that first morning and turned to look at her. She was still sleeping, not knowing that I was marveling at the progress being made in my life. She had no idea I was planning our wedding. I drove the short distance to work, giddy at the prospect of a life fulfilled.

Later that evening at rugby practice I was full of energy. I couldn't wait to slam into someone, feel the metal jump back from the collision. The testosterone surging through me was like electricity. Not completely over my "God's gift to the sport" ego, I was all over the court.

My energy was put to good use. Wendy Gumbert, our new coach, took no prisoners. We were a team that had not been to a national championship or a sectional playoff in seven years. She ramped up our practices and it was all we could do to keep up. She was building us up to be national contenders. I was building me up to soar in my independence. I was going to get married to Ruby.

My physical energy in the bedroom paralleled my physical energy on the court and I excelled with the Rolling Thunder. I attended all the practices and eagerly hung onto every word the coach said. I carried my inflated thinking through the practices. I remember Bill many times telling me, "Bob, you've got a lot to learn." I realize now he was talking about more than rugby.

Even though I had moved in with Ruby, I still wanted to go out and party with my teammates after practice and after the games. It was about seeing who could drink the most and how many girls you could meet. I wasn't much of a drinker but I loved to socialize. I felt myself going along with the crowd and doing what the culture of rugby, and sports in general, did at that time. My mindset was that it was okay. This was what athletes did. Ruby did not want to go out. She wanted to stay home, watch a movie, and eat pizza. She ran the show. She was not showing interest in getting married. She wanted to get back on her feet. She wanted a bigger house, more furniture. I went from being boyfriend to husband, dad, and financial partner without being married. She was more mature than I was. I went out and partied. I even had friends that were girls and we all went out.

"Go ahead; go out with your friends, even the girls. Just realize that if you have sex with them, I would know."

This caught me off guard. I was stunned into silence. How would she know?

"By the signal you'll give out, your body language. It will tell me everything I need to know."

Ruby had been married before and had had many other

relationships. She was full of emotional scars. She had been cheated on so she was clued in as to how cheating works and how the cheater husband behaves. I didn't do it because I would never cheat on a woman. I went out with other girls as friends but never crossed that line. I knew she would kick me out if I did, and rightfully so, so I stayed committed to her. I was just in over my head.

"Dude, she's just after you for your paycheck!" said Kurt during practice one day.

He wasn't the first one to say it. The subject had been raised many times when I was out on the town without her and during practices. I was beginning to see that maybe they were right. It was true, we had bought furniture together and I was paying my way with rent and groceries, but I only believed what she told me. I was enjoying the physical intimacy, and in that way she definitely loved me unconditionally, but the bottom line was that we were two people headed in different directions. It was becoming apparent that maybe it wasn't worth the trouble. I was learning some tough lessons from her. She had been through a lot and had developed a thick shield to keep around her. I always told her I wished she was more affectionate with me outside the bedroom. She did not like public displays of affection. I am a very affectionate person and like to show it. She would say to me, "don't tell me you love me; just say you like me a lot." It was all beginning to unravel. The plan wasn't working.

When I look at myself back then, I'm not sure what the allure was. I don't know what she would have been attracted to. She said it was the sincerity and the honesty and she needed that; it was something she wanted in a relationship. Maybe it was because I was young and immature; she could have her way with me, be above me. Maybe that was the attraction. I was wet behind the ears and she knew she could run the show, and she did. She pretty much laid it all out, handled all the finances, and made all the decisions. Looking back, I had it made; it was too perfect. But in the back of my mind I knew it was wrong to live with a girl I wasn't married to. It couldn't be right and we weren't moving in the positive direction I had first hoped. We argued and she would catch me being immature. "You're wrong; you're messing up," she would say after I failed to meet her expectations.

The financial agreement that started this whole mess in the first place began to crack. Even though I was paying my way, I currently was not making much money and it put a strain on Ruby's goal of more stuff. I hadn't yet landed in a career, partly because of my inability to communicate my strengths to my employers. Getting the job at the Paralympics had been easy but there was a whole different system to navigate in the world of regular jobs for the disabled. After a few months of selling urological supplies they let me go. I started bouncing from job to job.

God has a way of putting us into check; he humbles us in ways that sometimes we are not even aware of. Or, sometimes it's as obvious as a brick through a window. For me it was losing my job and working at no-where jobs that I was over qualified for, like telemarketer, or answering the phone taking pizza orders. It was humiliating to sit there with a graduate degree, and having worked at the second largest sporting event in the world, wondering where my career was. However, I would rather work at odd jobs and pay my own way than not work at all. I wasn't about to lose my independence after working so hard for so many years to gain it.

Telemarketing jobs came easy because I was just a voice. I was getting turned down for administrative and secretarial jobs because they couldn't, by law, ask me the "how" questions and I wasn't savvy enough yet to bridge the gap for them. I remember sitting in one office and the man across the desk from me looked at my resume, looked at my arms, and mostly stared at my resume in the hopes of finding something he could use to disqualify me for the job. He asked me a few questions about the Paralympics but he was mostly silent. I sat and waited for him to ask me the same questions he probably asked every other applicant, "What were your job duties, how long were you at this position, what were your reasons for leaving, etc.," but those questions never came. I could see he had questions but he knew that if he asked how I answer the phone, or if I can type or if I can hold and write with a pen, or put files together...he knew if he asked these questions he would be breaking the law.

Ruby came up with the idea to volunteer the information they could not ask me. This took some creativity. Sometimes I would call and say, "Hi, Mr. Smith, I just typed my new resume and I'm going to drive over and give it to you. I will be there in ten minutes." Then I would get in the car and drive to the office and hand him my resume. I would say, "Thank you, I will see you tomorrow for the interview." Or when I entered the interview office I would say, "I need to turn my phone off so we are not interrupted." This gave them a chance to see that I carry my own cell phone and that translates to using and answering their phones. I had to learn these skills after hearing so many no's. It just came down to ingenuity. I had to learn how to sell myself and find ways to make them comfortable and satisfy their insecurity.

Ruby stepped in and offered me a job working for her at the telephone company as a switchboard operator. Now she was my supervisor. This cemented her power in our relationship. I was grateful for the job but it wasn't a good move on a personal level. At the office she put on her supervisor hat and treated me as her subordinate, which I was. I had to realize what was going on; she had to do her job and give consequences if I was messing up. This played a mind trip on me. I had to learn to take it and not take it home with me. I knew this job wasn't going to be a career; I was just doing it for the paycheck, so I did what I had to do to survive.

So here I was working for her, under her, we were years apart, she didn't want to get married, she called all the shots and I worked just to work. I was suddenly lost and had no idea where I was going. The games had long since come and gone and everything seemed deflated, including my ego. I was the flying squirrel and the boyfriend who was being loved physically and financially, but not emotionally. Something had to give.

My spiritual life, or lack-there-of, suddenly came into sharp focus. How far had I fallen? What was I doing? Only a few of us have an experience like the Apostle Paul: Not having the proper knowledge or relationship with God and then *Bam!* God becomes the professed center of your life. But for me, I had had a deep relationship with God from childhood. Jesus had stood at the foot of my bed and asked me if I wanted to live or go home with Him. I chose to stay and live and had expected Him to give me a life. But it seemed that in the last few years I had run away from him like I never heard of him.

In that case I must be more like the Apostle Peter. I knew deep down inside that there was something better than this life I had created in Atlanta. I was sure that God hadn't brought me there to party my life away and live with a woman I wasn't married to. I was also sure that I had made many decisions that led me in the opposite direction of what He wanted for me. I hadn't yet learned that physical acceptance is not the way to gain validation for who I am as a person. I didn't see this until the mess became so big and I became so disenchanted with my lifestyle that I had nowhere to look for help but up.

I began to pray to God that He would lead me to a better job. Every break I had during the day I prayed, "Lord, lead me out of this job, out of this area, out of this relationship. Find a way for me." Over and over I prayed for several months. Finally, the day came when I received a call from the Lakeshore Foundation in Birmingham, Alabama. Kevin Orr, Youth Director and Assistant Athletic Director, was inviting me for a job interview. I was familiar with the organization because I had been there to play in tournaments with the Rolling Thunder. I was happy someone was calling *me* for once for an interview.

Ruby wished me luck and I drove to Alabama wondering if this was the answer I was praying for. During the 2 /12 hours it took me to get there, I thought a lot about my relationship with Ruby. She didn't seem shocked or upset that I was interviewing in a town 146 miles away. It didn't seem to faze her at all. I fantasized that she would come with me if I got the job, but in reality I wasn't sure if that was a good idea. Maybe I needed a clean break, to fully be out on my own with a real career. On the other hand, I didn't want to be alone. I wanted her to want me. I wasn't sure if she did.

My mind drifted back and forth, torturing myself with thoughts of wanting to leave her and wanting to stay, wanting her to come with me, and wanting to leave her behind. "Help me out, Lord." Finally, as I drove past the city limit sign for Birmingham, my mind snapped into interview mode and I began to rehearse how I would sell myself to prove I was a worthy candidate.

Unlike the times I had traveled to Lakeshore with the team,

this time, when I drove onto the 45-acre wooded campus, I had a sense of hope. As I turned into the drive I paid more attention to my surroundings, wondering if this was going to be my new home. The temperature was mild, the trees were colored in red and orange and the sun was shining through the leaves. It was a peaceful setting on a perfect fall day. The first building I passed was the Lakeshore Hospital and then the narrow blacktop road wound up through the trees and past the dormitories to the Wallace Gymnasium. Butterflies scattered in my stomach as I got out of the car and wheeled into the gym. Kevin Orr was waiting for me.

"Hello, Bob!" he said, smiling and extending his hand to shake my elbow from his wheelchair. "Welcome to Lakeshore!"

"Thank you! It's good to be here!" I said.

He asked about the traffic and I couldn't remember whether there had been traffic. "Good," I said and followed him down the hall to his office.

"Come on in," he said.

"Thank you. I typed a fresh copy of my resume," I said, taking it out of my bag and handing it to him.

He took it and immediately noticed I had a master's and was bilingual. He said he was impressed.

"Look. I'll get right to the point," he said. "Your credentials and job experience are excellent. I have no worries in that department. I've also seen you play rugby. I've watched how you've handled yourself on and off the court and I've noticed that you are self-sufficient. You're able to get around and take care of yourself with little or no help. As a Recreation Specialist, you would be in charge of the youth programs, working with kids with disabilities and their families. It's important to Lakeshore that we hire people that model our philosophy, not just here at the office but in life in general. Our mission is to enable people with physical disabilities and chronic health conditions to lead active, independent lifestyles through sports, recreation, and research. What I want to know is what message you give to people?"

"To do your best, don't let your disability slow you down, it doesn't define you; your attitude does, and your ability does. I've always tried to do my best. My goal has always been independence, no caretakers. I swim, play rugby and basketball."

"How did you lose your limbs?" he asked.

I gave him the short version of the story.

"And what about your family? How did they handle the transition?"

"They treated me like normal but my dad was adamant about me getting my education. He insisted I stay in regular classrooms. My family encouraged me to do the same activities that I did before my illness. I pretty much had a normal childhood. No special treatment. I had to do the work just like everyone else."

"I'm definitely looking for someone who has that attitude, to share that kind of image with the kids. It's important they have mentors to show them how to be independent. If we were to hire you, would you need any special equipment to help you do this job?"

"No sir. I can type 35 words per minute, I can use a pen, I can file, and I can use the telephone. I don't need any adaptable equipment," I replied.

We talked for a while longer about the Atlanta Rolling Thunder and the Lakeshore Demolition, the team I would join if I were offered the job. He took me on a tour of the facility, introduced me to the CEO and a few of the employees and then we parted.

"Thanks for coming in Bob. I'll get back to you in a week or two," he said.

As I drove away, I felt it had gone well. I began thinking about where I would live and if Ruby would come with me. Or maybe I needed to be brave and let her go. The next day at work my mind swirled. I realized even more that I was in a dead-end job and a dead-end relationship. I wanted to do more with my life than work a switchboard. I wanted to be with a woman who wanted to marry me, not control me and keep me for convenience.

A few weeks later, the call came from Lakeshore and I was offered the job.

"You have the full package of what we are looking for, Bob. You embody the image we want to portray here at Lakeshore. I'm offering you the job." Kevin paused.

"I accept!" I said, smiling into the phone.

"Great! When can you start?"

"Two weeks? I need to give notice at my job." Just then, my stomach formed a knot.

"Two weeks sounds great. We'll see you November 1."

The writing was on the wall with my relationship with Ruby when I told her I was moving to Birmingham and asked her if she wanted to come with me. She said no. In my mind, I felt this was God's way of saying *I'm bailing you out and giving you a better job. I'm moving you into a nicer area, where you will be working with good people, kids, and I'm taking you away from a relationship that has not been positive and not leading to marriage.*

The ultimate challenge for me was walking away from the one thing I had been waiting for my entire adult life, risking that it might never come my way again. I knew the relationship wasn't right so I had to use my head, against the wishes of my heart, to get out of it. I had to trust that God knew what He was doing. He was getting me out of this situation because I wasn't strong enough to do it on my own.

"But if you make yourselves at home with me and my words are at home in you, you can be sure that whatever you ask will be listened to and acted upon."

John 15:7 MSG

14

Born Again: Murderball

I T WAS HARD TO SAY goodbye to Ruby. In fact, I couldn't. I moved to Alabama and began working at Lakeshore, but technically we were still boyfriend and girlfriend. She came to visit me and I went back to visit her. We kept this long distance relationship for a few months, even though I knew it was wrong. I just didn't want it to end. I was afraid that there would never be another woman that would physically love me the way she did.

She was finally the one to break it off permanently. It hurt. I missed the intimacy. It was hard to be alone and let go of the person who first gave me unconditional love outside of my family. It didn't end badly, we were amicable, but I had a hard time letting her go. I tried to call or email from time to time but got no response. She always said that when she breaks up with someone, there is no more contact. That was her rule. But for a while, I couldn't obey it. I loved her very much. She will always hold a special place in my heart because she was the first woman to accept my broken body.

The move to Alabama was a step up in so many ways. My professional career launched on November 1, 1998, when I started as a Recreation Specialist at the Lakeshore Foundation. I rented an apartment close to work. I was in a new town, with a new job, on a new rugby team, and feeling all alone. I had to take stock of how far I'd fallen. I had to be man enough to admit I had come pretty far in a direction I should not have been going. Luckily I was in a pioneering town so I felt this was as good a place as any to make a fresh start.

The locals still refer to Birmingham as the Magic City, so named because it sprang up like magic in the 1870's after the railroad was put in. I was hoping it would add a little bit of magic to my life as well. I was also well aware that the state of Alabama has consistently produced some of our nation's most outstanding athletes: Hank Aaron, Bo Jackson, Mia Hamm, Carl Lewis, Charles Barkley, and Birmingham's own Willie Mays. I wanted to be one of them, and this became my focus.

It seems like an oxymoron to say I was born again from something called murderball, but that is exactly what happened when I joined the local club team, the Lakeshore Demolition. This was a new adventure to learn to be a better person and a better athlete; an *elite* athlete. Lucky for me, quad rugby is an intense, slam-fest of metal at a high rate of speed. While I was trying to regroup from losing Ruby and getting used to my new surroundings, I got out my frustration on the court by ramming my new teammates and pushing the wheels as fast as they would go.

The Lakeshore Demolition was among the top five club teams in the nation when I joined that fall. Club teams typically lean towards a recreational philosophy but an elite player must be a member of a club team in order to advance to a coveted spot on the National team. Like many other club teams, the Demolition was a mix of recreational and elite athletes. Brian Kirkland and Cliff Chunn were best-in-league players and were both 2.0 players. This meant that I was benched as soon as I became a member. This was a good thing. It gave me time to learn and develop as a player, as well as work on my ego. I got my head handed to me many times. They were better than me but I allowed myself to be coached and developed. This was a different team with different leadership, so I had to be different and exercise humility.

From day one, rugby practice with the Demolition was intense. It was a bone-jarring educational experience in how to play demolition rugby, all taught by the General: Kevin Orr. You can either jump on board with him or find yourself drifting out to sea. There wasn't any in-between. You were either in or out. Kevin Orr seemed to me like

Vince Lombardi, Bobby Knight and General Patton all rolled into one.

"Gather round, gentlemen. I would like to introduce Bob Lujano. Many of you are already familiar with him from the Atlanta Rolling Thunder. He's a 2.0 player and was recently hired here at Lakeshore," said Coach Orr with a loud voice, flipping through his notes. The players nodded in my direction but they were silent, obviously waiting for the coach to continue. I did a quick count: fourteen players including myself.

"We start our practices on time. There are no lazy people on this team! You need to be the best player you can be at all times, starting with and including today. This is a two-hour practice. We'll start with the usual 30 minutes of aerobic conditioning. Then we'll move on to passing drills, ball pickups, and a scrimmage at the end. Any questions?" Nobody said a word. He blew a loud whistle and the team scattered to the track around the gymnasium.

I quickly followed and fell into rhythm amongst a few of the players.

"Hi," said a guy near me with sandy brown hair and a boyish face. "I'm Tommy Sullivan. Everyone calls me Sully." He had an easy look about him.

Before I could respond, two other big dudes introduced themselves.

"How ya doing? I'm Willard and this is Brian."

"Good to meet you," I said holding out my arm.

"Speed up! This isn't a walk in the park! I don't want to see mediocrity; I want to see some speed. Move those wheels!" Coach Orr yelled across the gym. The team immediately did as they were told and I followed suit.

Exactly 30 minutes later Coach pulled us over to start drills. We started passing the ball to each other as we wheeled up and down the court. After a few clean throws and catches, one of the rock-hard covers I wear on both elbows flew off my arm. It went one way and the ball went the other.

"Dude, that hurts! Get that taken care of!" said a player I hadn't met yet.

"Throw the ball, not your prosthetic! Figure it out!" yelled Coach Orr.

Great. Day one and I'm already a target, I thought to myself. I erased that thought as quickly as it came and kept pushing the wheels. It takes time to settle in and relax, I told myself. I tried really hard that day to make a good first impression on my new team but it didn't go very well. I felt like a little kid again, up to bat with the bases loaded and dad in the stands watching. I tried so hard I struck out.

A week or so later after practice Coach Orr was letting us all have it. We were gathered around in a circle, exhausted and sweating, while he yelled about dropped passes and missed scoring opportunities. And then he turned his attention on me.

"You need to lose the spare tire, Bob! Lay off of those Twinkies and chocolate chip cookies! You need to get down the court in half the time! Speed is everything. You have quick arms but you need to improve your strength so you can go faster. If you want to be the best at this sport, then show it!"

It was yet another benchmark of approval I would need to meet.

"Junk in is junk out. It's about choices. It's about what you can and cannot control. What you put in your mouth is what you can control," he continued.

I listened intently. What a difference from Atlanta!

"As a person who lacks large muscle groups, you can't burn the calories like most people. If you drink beer and eat stupid food, you will gain stupid weight! You can't wheel as fast with that fat roll around your waist! I need you to be faster!"

And this was one of the easy days! My teammates didn't beat around the bush either. They joined right in as we did warm-ups. There is an unspoken philosophy on the court: If they're not bashing you, they don't really love you. That's how guys operate. It's all done out of love.

"Dude, are you gonna keep wearing those white under-armor t-shirts?" asked Brian.

"Looking sexy in those shirts, Bob!" said Willard.

I stepped up my game really fast. I was causing the wrong kind of attention. No more under-armor shirts and no more junk food. I started to take seriously the life of an athlete and what is expected of a top player. I changed my eating habits, stopped partying, and trained as hard as I could. After the many set-backs and let-downs in Atlanta from the dead-end jobs and rejection from Ruby, my ego had taken a big hit. I was humbled and ready to give up the life that was taking me nowhere. I was ready to embrace rugby for all it was worth to get my life back on track.

I reoriented my thinking back to the lessons of my father and decided that the day I stop wanting to be coached and yelled at is the day I will stop playing rugby.

When a player stops wanting to be coached he is saying two things: (1) I know everything, and (2) I don't need to listen to anyone but me. Once a player starts with this line of thought he is going downhill. He has stopped himself from growing and moving forward. I don't buy the saying that you can't teach an old dog new tricks. I think you can if the old dog can listen. If the old dog isn't deaf and hasn't built up enough pride and arrogance to purposely tune out the coach and his teammates, he can grow and improve. If a player reaches that point in life then he needs to stop playing. It hurts the team when players set themselves apart. I wasn't about to be one of those players.

During the games, the first issue I had to tackle (besides graduating from the bench) was staying in my chair. I was still known as the flying squirrel and the teams in my new league quickly picked up where the old league left off by taking every advantage to get me to fly out of my chair. News travels fast. I wasn't on the court very often, but when I was they rammed my chair as hard as they could to get me to fly. My new teammates were not happy about the turnovers this caused. They wanted a permanent solution to stop this from happening.

"Dammit Bob!" Coach Orr screamed across the court at me. "Stay in your chair! We don't want to know you like a bowling pin!"

During practice we finally came up with a NASCAR-like harness system, an over-the-shoulder seat belt, to keep me from falling out. This took the bulls-eye off my back during the games and dramatically reduced my time in the penalty box. I think I am the only player to ever use such a device. The other teams still slammed into me, because that's how the game is played, but once they knew they could no longer launch me, their focus shifted back to better strategies. The tension was also relieved from my teammates, who could now concentrate on scoring and defense rather than the liability every time I wheeled onto the court.

The second issue I needed to work on was protecting the ball. There is a technique called "reach in" which literally means to reach in and flick the ball off the opposing player's lap without touching the player. It's hard for me to reach in because my arms are too short. This means I am better at defense. My greatest weakness in rugby (amputee) is also my greatest strength (perfect spine). In other words, as an amputee, my lack of limbs is a hindrance to keeping me in my chair, or allowing me to reach in and flick, or catch high or wide balls. But because I am an amputee and do not have a spine injury like the rest of the players, I am able to twist my hips to make my chair move in ways they cannot. I am able to turn on a dime and speed away like lightning.

Coach Orr always preached to work with what we have and don't worry about the rest. He pushed me harder than the other players to finesse the skill of carrying the ball, using my hips and the strength in my back to protect the ball from the other team. It paid off. Very few people can get the ball from me.

As the weeks went on, the usual problems came up amongst the players: "I can't afford gas to get to practice." "Coach, can you give me some tires and tubes." "I don't have a ride." "I can't afford new equipment. Can you fix what I have?" "Can you loan me some tape?" I was used to hearing the dialogue, but Coach Orr's response was refreshing. It was the reason I was at Lakeshore; he embodied the philosophy of independence and brought it to the court.

"Gimme, gimme, gimme! That's all I hear from you guys! Why don't you get off your lazy butts and go out and get a job! Don't be a bump-on-a-log, be a human. Don't just be an athlete, be a well-rounded person. Society doesn't expect anything from you, but I do. Just because you're a quadriplegic doesn't mean you can't go out and live life to the fullest. Get off disability. Go to school. Get a job so you can afford a car and gasoline and equipment. Find a girlfriend and get married and have kids. Stop this gimme, gimme crap! And while we're on the subject, how about getting to practice on time? And if you do have jobs, get to work an hour early so you're not coming in here late!"

That kind of frustrated tirade only meant one thing: a harder workout. It translated to faster laps around the track, higher requirements for drills, and tougher scrimmages. His philosophy was that we were no different than anybody else. He didn't want us to listen to the message society places on the disabled that we need to be taken care of because we can't take care of ourselves. This is nonsense, Coach Orr would say over and over again. He told us that when we succeed in rugby we succeed in life, and when we succeed in life we succeed in rugby. He didn't want us to win championships and then go back to bed and wait to be taken care of. He wanted us to win championships and then go do life to the fullest like regular people.

We heard him loud and clear and took him up on his challenge. Not because he was yelling at us but because he believed in us. I am fortunate that from day one my family believed in me and pushed me to integrate into the able-bodied world; Coach Orr's message and belief that we could achieve was not new to me. For some of the players though, it was the first time anyone had believed in them. It was the first time since their accidents that someone actually had the gumption to tell them to get away from the TV and go *do* something. When someone close to you, like a coach, gives you this gift it is life changing.

I was invited to a training camp that year to be considered for a spot on Team USA that would travel to Christchurch, New Zealand for the World Wheelchair Games. In fact, all the Lakeshore players were at this camp as well as players from club teams across the United States. We were all vying for a spot on the national team. Suddenly, there was competition instead of camaraderie. Everyone was silently choosing the lineup and I was being counted out. There was uneasiness about my capabilities.

Having me as a teammate on a club team was one thing, but at the international level it was quite another story. The players from across the country didn't trust my lack of limbs. They didn't know me or my capabilities. During one particular scrimmage I wheeled up and down the court but I was never given the ball. Coach Orr had been chosen as the head coach of the national team and was starting to boil as the players continued to ignore me. This worked to my benefit during a crucial moment of the camp. He knew what I could do, but he needed the other players to believe in me as well.

"Throw him the ball!" coach yelled. They looked at him but passed it to someone else.

I was open, I was quick to get myself in position but they kept throwing the ball to each other.

Finally, Coach Orr had enough. He blew an angry whistle, slammed his clipboard down onto the floor and everything stopped.

"Gather round!" he screamed as he wheeled red-faced onto the court. We quickly formed a circle. Even the players that were not yet used to him knew this was one moment that wasn't going to be good if we didn't listen immediately.

"Give me the ball!" he yelled again. One of the players tossed him the ball and without even looking at me, he chucked the ball as hard as he could at me. I caught it. He motioned for me to throw it back. I wasn't sure where he was going with this.

"Bob is a class 2 player! He's supposed to be a ball carrier! Throw him the ball!" And he whipped it as hard as he could in my direction again without looking at me. I caught it and threw it back.

"You think because he doesn't have arms that he can't catch the ball?" The ball flew back to me at warp speed. He was taking some serious venom out on that thing. I caught it and threw it back.

"You guys should know more than *anybody*," and now he was looking and pointing at each player in turn, "that discrimination is based on face value! And right here in Wheelchair Rugby, we fight against that! You know you can do more than what people give you credit for! People dismiss you just by looking at you! And now you are doing it to Bob? I hear you mumbling in the background that he can't do this or that!" The ball shot back to me like a bullet. I caught it and threw it back.

"So you're just going to go with this? He only has arms to his elbows so you're not going to give him the ball? Are *you* going to decide for *him* what he can and cannot do? Carry your own load! Don't worry about Bob, he can catch it!" Once again, with all his anger and might he hurled the ball. I caught it and threw it back.

"Throw him the ball!" One last time, with crushing force, he chucked the ball so hard at me I thought it might knock me out of my harness. But I caught it, thank God, and threw it back. He put the ball on his lap and wheeled back to the sidelines.

We all sat there, not sure what to do next. My face burned with embarrassment, but I was so grateful that he stood up for me. The players sat stunned for a moment while they soaked it in. I knew they were also embarrassed but for a different reason. They got the point that their attitude towards me was off, that deciding I was a lesser player incapable of international competition was a form of discrimination. As men who are disabled, they had their own challenge of being overruled thrown back in their faces; they were using discrimination towards me the same way they had been discriminated against out in the world.

Fortunately for me, they were impressed with the ability I displayed in that impromptu exercise. So much so, in fact, that as the days went on they harassed me with a new respect when I messed up.

"Hey Bob, I thought you could catch anything?" Brian teased.

"He can't catch a cold!" laughed Sully.

But I knew their teasing meant I was in. I had proved I could keep up with them without arms. The point was made and the pressure was on. They accepted me as a member of the national team and realized I was a serious player. They could count on me to get the job done.

Three of fourteen Demolition players made the national team. We traveled to New Zealand in October that year for the world games. It was my first overseas competition. It was a sixteen-hour flight from L.A. to Auckland but I didn't care. It could have been sixteen days and I would not have complained. I was just glad to be on the U.S. team and going overseas. I was anxious and excited but didn't want to mess up or disappoint my team or my family. I just wanted to play rugby and enjoy being in another country...and most importantly, win the gold medal.

We did win the gold by beating the New Zealand Wheelbacks in front of their home crowd. Fortunately for us yanks, New Zealand did not hold a grudge. We were treated graciously and with great hospitality. The best part of New Zealand was being there during the able-bodied Rugby World Cup championship and to see the city embrace rugby, including wheelchair rugby.

After winning gold at the World Games, the players that made up the national ensemble were considered the up and coming talent for U.S. Rugby. Coach Orr set a high standard for the national team and kept that standard for the Lakeshore Demolition. He gave both teams a system to buy into: accountability with each other. He preached to us the concept of unity; how we act on and off the court as individuals is very important to the overall success of the team. He drilled into us that how we carry ourselves on and off the court, how we play, how we live, says a lot about who we are as people, not just players. All he needed to say to me was, "Bob, there is a brick wall, go run through it," and I would do it. To have a coach who leads by example is great. It is easy to follow someone who is unselfish and makes the commitment themselves.

During the off-season I continued to push up the hills, forward and backwards, to improve my cardio. I watched what I ate and kept my weight down so I would be ready to go for the next season and not have to start training from scratch. This got the CEO of Lakeshore, Jeff Underwood, in a bit of a pickle. He was returning from lunch with one of the board members, Bill Acker, who is a single-leg amputee, and they witnessed me pushing up the hill in my chair.

"Jeff, why aren't you providing closer parking spaces for your disabled employees?" asked a wide-eyed Bill.

"I do. They're right there in front of the building. That's Bob Lujano. He chooses to park down the hill in the employee lot to keep the blue spaces open for the patrons."

"For real?" asked Bill.

"Yes," laughed Jeff. "He's for real. Besides being a real gentleman, he's also one of our rugby players. I think he likes the exercise."

I saw them watching me and Jeff relayed the conversation to me after Bill left. But that wasn't the only time I was being talked about. There was a conversation that took place after the ball incident between Coach Orr and Jeff Underwood.

"How is Bob Lujano doing?" asked Jeff.

"He's doing just fine. Is there a reason you're asking?" said Kevin.

"I trust your judgment, Kevin. I'm not second-guessing your decision to hire him. I've seen him around and I'm impressed with what I see. But there have been questions about safety with him interacting with the kids, because he's missing his limbs. Do you have any concerns?"

"If I had concerns I wouldn't have hired him. As his coach and his boss, I see a lot of Bob and I can tell you that he is good at both work and rugby. I've watched him with the kids and he's great with them. The beauty with him is that he has no limits. He's smart and he's adapted very well to using what he has. He just adapts. It's all part of the package of who Bob is. He's not rugby Bob, or employee Bob, or spiritual Bob; he is the same guy in all situations. I can challenge a guy like that. He doesn't break. Successful at sport means successful at work with the kids. I have no qualms at all with him. Is there someone complaining?"

"No. No one is complaining," said Jeff. "It's just been brought up that maybe there *should* be a concern."

"No, there should not be a concern. In fact, let me tell you what happened a few weeks ago in practice," said Kevin, and he relayed how he got mad at the players for not trusting me with the ball and then chucking it at me to prove his point that I can catch it.

"That example to the team could have gone all wrong. We didn't rehearse; he didn't know what was coming. He could easily have dropped the ball. But he didn't. He caught it and did what he needed to do. The difference between successful people and not, is that they make the plays when they need to. Adversity will make you crumble or lift you up. Bob always makes the play when he needs to. He looks fear in the eye and says, 'I'm going to beat you.' That's why he's successful. He can take the heat and make things happen. I'm harder on him than the other players because I can be; the guy is unflappable! He takes it as a challenge and steps up his game every time."

"Fair enough," said Jeff. "I thought so, but I just wanted to be sure."

"Anything else?" asked Kevin.

"Nothing else." said Jeff.

Once again, Coach Orr to the rescue. I wasn't aware of that conversation until years later. He never gave me special treatment, I had to work harder than the others to earn my spot, but he always stood up for me. He stood up for all of us.

At the start of our second rugby season, Coach Orr decided to take things up a notch for the Lakeshore Demolition. At that time there was still a mix of recreational and elite athletes on the roster. Some of the elite athletes were driving two hours just to get to practice. Coach Orr realized how serious some of these players were so he catered to their goals to make them the best-of-the-best. He made the announcement on our first day back.

"I'm gonna take you guys to the woodshed. Make it really hard. Practices will be extended from two hours to three hours. The cardio and muscle building will be hour-long pushes up and down the hills and we'll ramp up the drills."

We got together as a team behind the Coach's back.

"Do we really need to do hour long pushes? Three hour practices? It seems like too much."

The up-and-coming national players were ready to meet the challenge but the recreational players were not so sure they wanted to make this type of commitment. Ultimately, as a team, we agreed, outside of Coach Orr, that we would do it. The elite players stepped up their game but eventually some of the recreational players couldn't hang on and didn't think they would advance to national level even if they could make it through the grueling workouts. Several of them left the team. It was the weeding out of the boys from the men. Coach Orr could do this because he had talented players who wanted gold. He pushed us hard to see who wanted it the most. We were soon living up to our name, demolishing everyone in our path.

Coach Orr lived up to his word. Those early days were a lot like boot camp. We started off with conditioning; mile pushes forwards and backwards up and down the hills on the Lakeshore campus, timed pushes around cones, long passing drills, game strategies and situations. We would only scrimmage for about 20 minutes. None of us wanted to be the weakest member of the team. Mistakes would result in the entire team having to push more laps or sprints, which came with glaring looks to the offender as if he committed a crime. But it also tested our will and desire. If as a team we could survive an intense practice without hating each other, then the game would be anti-climactic. This was very much the case. We demolished many of our opponents because we were better conditioned and better coached.

We had many games won within the first four minutes. We had so much speed, depth, and talent that opposing teams knew they didn't stand a chance. We could see it in their eyes and in their play. I remember one game we were ahead of a team 33-0 at halftime and the team didn't come out for the second half. It was complete domination. This was the only time I knew of that a team actually quit. Soon, our reputation spread as a fast and physical team. But according to Coach Orr, it isn't just about winning; it is winning to your potential.

The most difficult games were when we played a team that was ranked much lower than ours. If we were capable of winning by a 20-goal margin, then we better do it. If we only won by ten, then according to Coach Orr, we were slacking off and that earned you a seat on the bench, right beside the coach. With the talent we had, we first had to check our egos at the door. Each of us had to realize that if we didn't give maximum effort and improve our play, then we would see many games from the sideline.

Eventually we dominated rugby by winning five consecutive USQRA National Championships ('99-'03) and had eleven total championship appearances. No other team in the twenty five year history of the league has come close.

By 2002 I was ready to advance to the next level of elite athlete. Being a member of Team USA is not automatic from year to year. We have to try out on an annual basis, just like any other sport. I had been chosen five years in a row, but this time, earning a spot on the national team meant early preparation for the 2004 Paralympics. The Paralympic team roster wouldn't be picked for another year, there were several hurdles to jump through to get to that point, but being on the 2002 national team was an important step in that direction. We were being groomed for gold! I salivated with excitement at the thought of my athletic dreams coming true. It was now within reach. My hard work was paying off!

Our journey to the Paralympics ended up being recorded for the documentary *Murderball* by Dana Adam Shapiro and Henry Rubin. They showed up at training camp where we were preparing for the 2002 World Wheelchair Championships. They brought in a camera and began filming everything and anything we did. We weren't sure what this was all about. They followed us to the IWRF World Competition in Sweden.

As a team, we had the physical skills and abilities to win the gold but there was more going on than just skills and abilities. The back-story between the Canadians and the Americans was deep and the animosity followed us from this game all the way to the Paralympics.

Much of the sport today is because of the Canadians; they invented it and the United States perfected it. A man named Joe Soares was considered the best quad rugby player in the world in 1996. I watched him play for Team USA in the exhibition games at the Paralympics in Atlanta. With his own unique personality, he was the Michael Jordan of quad rugby; a macho and charismatic leader. He was good and he knew it; a lot of smack came out of his mouth. But after the 1996 Para's in Atlanta, he lost some of his speed and sharpness and was cut from Team USA. He brought a lawsuit, complaining he was unfairly cut. It didn't go very far. He applied to be a coach but he had burned so many bridges with the lawsuit that they did not accept him. So he went to coach the Canadian team, taking our plays and philosophies with him. Some of the American players called him a traitor to his country.

The first time Team USA competed against the Canadians with Joe Soares as their coach was at the World's in 2002. To say it was tense is an understatement. There was a lot of bad blood that had been spilled in the controversy and this was the first time he would face his former teammates. We stepped up the intensity and did not back down to him. Coach Orr was adamant that we answer him on the court, not to his face. Soares talked a lot of smack. His attitude was reflective of the entire Canadian team that year: bravado and arrogance. This game wasn't so much about rugby and nationalism as it was about honor and revenge.

Our mental game fell apart and we lost the gold medal to Team Canada, 25-24. In that game, there was no positive spin. We did not celebrate "winning the silver." No. We lost the gold…to Joe and his Canadians. The film crew for the documentary had gotten it all on tape. Great. We were distracted, we were angry, and we let outside influences keep us from doing the job we knew we could do.

As soon as the World's finished, Rubin and Shapiro put an article in Maxim Magazine in November of 2002, about "Murderball." The article was met with success so they moved full steam ahead to film every training camp, every practice, and every clinic in preparation for the 2004 Paralympics in Athens. It was then we realized this was a serious venture. We saw their commitment and knew something special was going to happen. For two-and-a-half years, they filmed us, hung out with us, played cards, and pulled each one of us aside for interviews; basically trying to get to know each one of us personally.

After our loss to Canada, Coach Orr brought in Dr. James Hilyer, Sports Psychologist, to help us with our mental game. Dr. Hilyer has worked with such teams as the Washington Redskins and the New Orleans Saints; this was serious. No more losses due to mental breakdowns. We were licking our wounds and practicing angry when he came to work with us. If we were to have a chance at success in the Paralympics, we needed to get our act together. We were not accustomed to letting our guard down. We were in the business of demolition. The hard work that had gotten us to the gold medal round quickly fell apart in the volatile atmosphere of questioned loyalty, drama, and revenge.

Dr. Hilyer worked with us as a team and as individuals to up our game. He showed me to use mental imagery to learn to place the ball wherever I wanted it. I needed to be able to bump the ball (like in volleyball) right into a players lap. Rugby is so fast that I don't want to make my teammate lose precious time by reaching for the ball and then putting it in their lap when I pass it to them. I want to place it right into their lap so they can keep wheeling with little interruption.

Dr. Hilyer had me visualize this technique over and over until I was able to place the ball exactly where I wanted it.

I found I was still Shooter, only now at the elite level.

In June of 2003, two pivotal events, The North American Cup tournament and the U.S. Paralympic Quad Rugby Tryouts, were held the same week at The Lakeshore Foundation in Birmingham. I competed with the Demolition in the tournament and I attended the camp to try out for the team that would represent the U.S. at the Paralympics. This was a hard five days of double duty and I was dead-dog tired. We had put in grueling nine-hour workouts between the tryouts and the competitions. Most people don't understand the amount of work it takes to be a Paralympian. People assume that because we are in chairs, and are competing in the "Paralympics" and not the "real" Olympics, that a spot on the team just gets handed to us. The assumption is that it's easier somehow, that it isn't a real competition like the Olympics. I, and all the other athletes vying for a spot, have to work just as hard as Michael Phelps. We have to put in the work just like he does to earn our spot.

At the end of the five days, the selection committee for the Paralympics called us to order. We sat silently sweating it out, waiting for our name to be called: Lynn Nelson, Clifton Chunn, Wayne Romero, Brent Poppen, Will Groulx, Scott Hogsett, Andy Cohn, Norma Lyduch, Bryan Kirkland, Mark Zupan, Sam Gloor, and Bob Lujano. YES! I was chosen as a member of Team USA! I was going to the Paralympics as a competitor! My dream at the age of nine to be an elite athlete had been handed back to me. I was being given another chance. I couldn't wait to call my dad, my sister, my Grandma Hope, and let them know that another dream was being realized. I wouldn't be playing for the Cincinnati Reds but playing for Team USA in the Paralympics was equally sweet and just as much an accomplishment.

At the end of the next day, the final day of the tournament, I was about at my limit of exhaustion when something happened. We had just won the North American Cup over Canada (sweet revenge!) and the gym was packed with people: there were teams that had lost earlier in the competition that stayed to watch the last game, local residents, employees of Lakeshore, and players who had tried out for the Paralympics had all stayed to watch the trophy round between the two countries who were still bickering. In the chaos and revelry of the win, kids from a local school gathered around me after the game. I had visited them two weeks prior to talk about my job at the Lakeshore Foundation, show them my physical abilities, and eat pizza with them and had invited them to come and watch the competition. As the film crew for *Murderball* stood off to the side and filmed the kids congratulating me on my successful week, all of the sudden this boy asks me,

"How do you eat pizza with your elbows?"

Even though he had witnessed me doing it at his school, his young brain still couldn't get it straight how this was possible and he wanted answers. I always try to answer questions politely and graciously, especially when they come from kids. In fact, I encourage questions. But complete physical and mental exhaustion had set in. I had nothing left. Out of the 500 or so quad rugby players in the country, I was one of twelve who had proved during the week I was a Paralympian inside and out, headed to the biggest athletic stage in the world. On top of that, our club team had just won the national tournament. I was now an elite athlete and this boy wanted to know how I feed myself? Whoosh. I was right back to the reality of a limbless man. How, how, how? How do you do this, how do you do that?

I chuckled, and said, "like this," raising the file folder I was holding to demonstrate how I bring food to my mouth but right at that moment it all caught up to me—the fatigue, the realization of a life-long goal, the self-assurance of knowing "I am able" coupled with the frustration that society will always view me as "dis" abled—it all came rushing in, choking me, and I was suddenly overwhelmed with emotion. Out of instinct I turned away from him so he wouldn't see my vulnerability. His question caught me off guard because I was suddenly thrown into the opposite extremes of my life. The gym was filled with euphoria and relief and accomplishment. It was noisy. I was dripping with the kind of sweat that comes from the fruit of your labor, the kind you aren't ready to wash off because you want to savor the feeling of finally holding your dream in the palm of your hand. And yet I had to explain a basic human function of feeding myself.

I was a Paralympian showing what I had learned as a child, a basic function everyone else has the pleasure of taking for granted. It was surreal and I started to lose my composure.

"I'm okay, its okay," I said quickly, my voice catching in my throat, my eyes searching the floor as I fiddled with my chair.

But in my heart I was ready to cry. *Really?* I had just accomplished so much. I don't begrudge the boy. He was just curious. And I was just bone tired. It was all caught on tape and put into the documentary.

After the game the film crew for *Murderball* asked to come to my house to watch how I did things. I thought, *Great. First the boy and now the crew with the same question...How?* I was so tired but I realized they were doing something unique so I agreed. They filmed me using my keys to unlock the front door of my house, load the dishwasher, get in my van, pour a glass of juice, etc. But we also had a chance to talk and open up. They are talented and kind; not exploitative or yelling about photo-ops. They were very driven but quiet and supportive, so I had no issue working with them. I remember asking why they wanted me to be a part of this. There were eleven other guys on the team. They said, "You have a different disability and something about you is different from the other guys." I took this as a compliment. I very much enjoyed the whole experience.

The next year, in 2004, The North American Cup had a different tone to it. Many different countries participated as a way to be seeded in the upcoming Paralympics. Team USA won the tournament, over Canada, which meant we were ranked as #1 in the world heading into the Para's in Athens, Greece!

The pomp-and-circumstance of a Paralympian is exciting. The red, white, and blue uniforms arrived, official pictures were taken, and I was giddy on the twelve-hour flight that my life had come full circle. I was realizing a dream. I had worked hard to achieve this elite athlete status and I envisioned bringing home the gold for me, my teammates, my family, and my country. We all did. My teammates had the same vision and we were determined to get the job done.

My dad and step-mom travelled to Athens with Lisa, her son Brent, and my cousin Paul. Participating in the opening ceremonies was one of the proudest and most profound experiences of my life. I wasn't behind the scenes organizing the volunteers this time; I was an athlete. It was great to have my family there to share this accomplishment. The team anxiously waited in line for three-and-a-half hours for the program to start, and then it took an hour-and-a-half for our team to enter the stadium in the parade of athletes. It was thrilling.

The American flag escorted our group onto the track and we began our walk around the stadium. The crowd cheered and took pictures and we could not wipe the smiles from our faces. This was it. We had arrived. I could not help notice the 85-foot tall olive tree in the center of the stadium, surrounded by green grass. It was to symbolize life. How appropriate that a tree of *life* would be the symbol at the Paralympics in which I was an athlete.

Quad Rugby, Murderball, had in many ways given me a part of my life back that I thought was gone forever. I was living more life than I ever thought possible through this sport and I was so grateful to God that He had brought me to this place. I marveled at the tree as the lights turned it red and then blue and I soaked in the life it was giving. It was a phenomenal moment. The fireworks lit up the stadium and the tree of life stood shining in all its glory. I thanked God for this moment and for the life he had given me. And I thought, *I am so blessed.*

A couple of days later we started the week-long journey to gold. Instead of 60 or 80 people in attendance at a home game at Lakeshore, there were 5000 people in attendance to watch the rugby tournament. We were nervous, to say the least. As players, we were the main event. The crowd was there to watch heavy competition so we were aware that we could not bring our B game, we had to bring our A game. We beat Japan, 54-39; we beat New Zealand, 35-32; and we beat Australia, 49-38 in the preliminaries. In the quarterfinals, we beat Germany 46-34. In the semi-finals, we faced Team Canada.

For some of the guys, who had not had the benefit of being with Dr. Hilyer, it was still Joe Soares vs. USA, not Canada vs. USA, and this high-pressure game got to them a little. We came out flat right away but managed to be up one point at halftime with possession of the ball. Team Canada came barreling back, we had a possession error and they tied the score. Our attitudes changed dramatically. One of our players had a flagrant foul which put him out for three offensive plays and now we were down three points in the third quarter. Team Canada played keep away in the fourth quarter and we couldn't gain ground. A few of our guys were still learning how to win, the chemistry wasn't solidified yet and we couldn't pull it together. The cameras for *Murderball* were also a bit of a distraction. We lost the semi-final game 24-20 and our chance to play for gold. We lost as a team. It wasn't one person's fault. Joe Soares was euphoric. The top three teams were all 4 and 1. We had one bad game. It wasn't the right time to have a bad game. A three-minute breakdown turned the game sideways and that was that. Goodbye gold.

We played Great Britain for the bronze medal. It's hard to shift gears from a loss like that but it shows the character of the team. The unique element of our team is that we always bounce back. I'll never forget the equipment guy on the bus. He said, "This team is never going to be together again. Let's go show them what we are made of." This got us fired up. We responded to the loss with a win. We won the bronze medal, 43-39. We also smiled at Team Canada's loss to New Zealand in the gold medal round, 31-29.

Personally, I was very grateful for the bronze medal. I had worked very hard to make the U.S. Paralympic Rugby Team. I am very thankful to be one of 88 U.S. Paralympic athletes out of 300 to bring home a medal. However, at the time, this sentiment was not being shared by my teammates and coaches. I understood. I too felt their pain. I too felt as if we had underachieved. We felt as if we had disappointed our families, especially those family members who traveled around the world to see us play. I felt as if we had disappointed our sponsors. Men who worked tirelessly to fundraise for our Paralympic rugby team, who had to convince corporate sponsors to invest in this sport called murderball. I felt as if we had disappointed our country.

Wearing red, white and blue is not just a novelty. It's an honor and a privilege. Most importantly, I felt as if I had disappointed our coaches and staff, who put in countless and thankless hours of work and sacrifice. Their efforts can never be accurately measured. I will never forget Nancy Lehrer, Jane Thomas, James "Gumbie" Gumbert, Ed Suhr, Wendy Gumbert, John Bishop, Marty Frierson, Kelly Butler, and Coach Orr for their commitment and effort. Thank you is not a big enough phrase.

The filmmakers for the documentary *Murderball* had gotten it all on tape, the whole Paralympic experience. By the time they finished, after we won the bronze medal in Greece, they had 200 hours of footage to condense to an 85-minute film. What an amazing job they did. It was released in theaters in 2005 and was nominated for an Oscar for Best Documentary. It won two awards at the Sundance Film Festival for Best Documentary, along with several other wins and nominations at other festivals. All of the sudden, it was my turn to be Brad Pitt! It was a moment in the sun for me and my teammates. We were on radio shows and TV shows in New York and Los Angeles. The big one was *Larry King Live*. I couldn't believe I was sitting there with some of my teammates, Andy Cohn, Mark Zupan, Keith Cavill, and Scott Hogsett, across the table from Larry King! That was an amazing hour of life.

I have to admit though, that the documentary is a little rough. Not everyone was happy with the way we were portrayed. Some of the players and members of the wheelchair athlete community were upset at being shown as "a bunch of skirt chasers." The language is rough, the content is rough, but it is a beautiful documentary. Joe Soares was one of the more outspoken dissenters of the movie. He was so upset about his onscreen appearance that he threatened to sue.

All I can say is that for those of us who were privileged enough to be featured in *Murderball,* we are who we are and I think the producers did an excellent job of capturing each of us as individuals. The film did what it set out to do, "crash stereotypes" about the disabled community. We proved on camera that we can work, play elite sports, live independently, and be productive citizens in an able-bodied world. I'm very proud of this.

"When I kept it all inside, my bones turned to powder, my words became daylong groans. The pressure never let up; all the juices of my life dried up. Then I let it all out; I said, 'I'll make a clean breast of my failures to God.' Suddenly the pressure was gone—my guilt dissolved, my sin disappeared."

Psalm 32:3-5 MSG

15

The Emotionally Challenged

B OB'S STORY SAT DORMANT ON my desk for a year-and-a-half after that visit in Birmingham. I just couldn't see the truth that was right in front of me. Or, more accurately, I didn't want to accept it.

The truth is that Bob has figured out that a meaningful life isn't measured by circumstances or situations. A life of purpose isn't dependent on what we were given physically. Value isn't given through status or credentials. It's accepting and overcoming whatever challenge is in front of you with integrity and wisdom that gives meaning and purpose.

I did a lot of soul-searching in those 18 months, desperate to figure out why he was okay and I wasn't. I poured over the manuscript for clues. The first hint of an answer was the obvious difference between our families and how we were raised. Bob and I were living in the opposite extremes of life. After his amputations, his family quickly transitioned; he learned early on that he didn't need two arms and two legs to live a life of substance. I learned early on that getting through life was all about pretense and physical appearance; just look good and don't cause a fuss. Bob was taught to fly without the aid of limbs. I was kept under control. Bob was taught to push to new heights. I was kept from trying for fear I would fail. Hard work was expected from Bob. Very little was expected of me.

That's why I reacted the way I did when we met at St. Mary's. I was shocked because I couldn't fathom that a deep-seated joy could come from a body that was so flawed. The thought of taking away my physical tools to get through life frightened me because that's all I was taught to use to get by. That's why I went on a fact finding mission to his home in Birmingham because I wondered how he could be happy living beyond the aesthetic. I didn't trust his gratitude because I thought I had what he didn't, yet I was full of anger. Why wasn't he?

My own shallowness and the emptiness I felt was keeping me in a life of naval gazing. I wasn't fully living; I was existing in a defensive posture.

Bob was not in denial as I originally suspected, but he *was* living in a way that was unthinkable to me. He was living a life of freedom, of gratefulness, of humility, of real love for others and I couldn't understand it because I was shackled, waiting for the next traumatic circumstance to emerge.

Why was freedom so unthinkable? What was it I couldn't put my finger on?

Another hint came when one day out of frustration I re-read the large stack of newspaper articles written about him. One theme stood out loud and clear: his belief vs. everyone else's *disbelief.* The headlines in the seventeen years between Kansas, Texas, Tennessee, and across state lines through the National Enquirer sounded the same no matter the year or the paper: "…achieves goals despite disability… middle name is courage…gutsy teen beats odds to graduate…no arms or legs but lots of guts…beating adversity…has excelled despite rare childhood illness…" I recognized the ugly undertone: we didn't expect him to. We think if a man has his limbs removed, well, that must mean his life is over. He's out of the game.

That's why the newspapers were unanimous in calling him inspirational, because he kept going despite the struggle and daily public reaction. Bob wants to eat pizza and chicken wings at restaurants and get a proper education and work and pay bills and watch and play sports and suntan at the beach and participate in social change and teach and love and take care of himself just like everyone else. So he does, regardless of the how in getting there.

But to get an answer bigger than his upbringing and more

meaningful than his refusal to be held back, I had to go back to Bob's beginning and ask *what am I missing*. He was physically abused by his dad and grandpa, abandoned by his mother, ravaged with disease, and half of his body was taken away, and yet given the chance to be rid of all that and go to heaven, he chose to stay. He chose the pain, the scars, and the brokenness. *Why? How?*

A closer look at his encounter with Jesus finally gave me the long awaited answer.

Jesus stood at the foot of Bob's hospital bed after he had lost everything and asked a question. *Do you want to live or come home with me?*

I think there was more on the table than a simple offer of a ride home.

Jesus was offering Bob something far, far greater than saying, *Yeah, you've been through a lot, and if you want to come home with me it's no problem*. If Bob would have answered *I have had enough, take me home*, I believe Jesus would have lovingly wrapped him in His arms and welcomed him with gladness.

It was bigger than that. Jesus was making Bob an unbelievable offer.

I believe Bob's soul intrinsically knew that the life Jesus offered was unlike anything he had previously experienced.

Somewhere deep in the recesses of his comatose state, Bob's soul recognized the life giving Spirit standing before him. Not that life would suddenly be easy, not that his limbs would miraculously grow back, not that people wouldn't stare or discriminate, not that he wouldn't struggle with relationships or careers, not that he wouldn't have to keep proving himself over and over. No. Jesus was offering something so radical it had to be spoken from the Spirit to his soul.

Jesus offered to take his broken limbs and assemble them into purpose and passion. He offered to touch the scars on his face and body and beautifully arrange them into strength and courage. He offered to take the shame from the physical abuse and redeem his mindset to a place of peace and joy. He offered to take the rejection and abandonment from his mom and transform these emotions into grace and compassion for others.

This was the offer of *life* from Jesus.

Bob believed Jesus. He accepted His offer by saying *I want to live, I have things to do.* He didn't understand at the time what those "things" were, but now, looking back, we can see clearly the impact of the transaction that day.

Bob's original passion for sport transpired into a purpose through quad rugby. His strength and courage allows him to participate in the daily rituals of life with pride. The peace and joy in his soul give restful nights of sleep; God has his back and he needn't worry about tomorrow. The grace and compassion pours into his occupation, leading by example an independent life despite missing his limbs. These were the "things" Bob had to do.

Bob is grateful for the life Jesus gave him. We only need to look at the totality of his life to witness the evidence of Jesus' promises fulfilled in Bob. It's inarguable.

Jesus said: *"You did not choose me, but I chose you and appointed you so that you might go and bear fruit [love, joy, peace, patience, kindness, goodness, gentleness, faithfulness, and self-control]." John 15:16 & Galatians 5:22 NIV*

Gratitude is not a part of the list of fruit from the Holy Spirit. That's because gratitude is a choice. It is something we can control on our end. When we choose gratitude, it is as if we are fertilizing the soil of our soul. Once fertilized, the fruit—love, joy, peace, patience, kindness, goodness, gentleness, faithfulness, self-control—can grow within us. We don't have to try harder to be peaceful or kind or patient. It floods in and grows by the Spirit when we accept Jesus' offer and choose to live in gratitude for the life of freedom He gives us. Jesus makes this offer to all of us, not just Bob.

Bob *chose* his life. After all the tragedy he had been through and then given the choice to live on earth or go home to paradise with Jesus, *Bob chose to stay and do life.* That's why he never complains and is grateful for everything because Jesus made good on his offer of a radical life, something he had never experienced and couldn't imagine being possible. Bob's gratitude for life itself has grown more spiritual fruit than anyone I know.

The surface things of life—jobs, money, loss, possessions, errands, relationships, talents, passions, education, sports, sickness—these are all the tools and opportunities to live out the kind of life Jesus offers.

Bob's cross to bear is to walk each of us through this lesson, one slice of pizza at a time.

*"You keep me going when times are tough—my bedrock, God,
since my childhood. I've hung on to you from the day of my birth,
the day you took me from the cradle; I'll never run out of praise.
Many gasp in alarm when they see me, but you take me in stride."*

Psalm 71:4-7 MSG

16

Worlds Collide

WHEN I RETURNED WITH MY bronze medal to Birmingham after the Paralympics and the movie tour, I had a deeper perspective of my path in life. The goal of *Murderball* became my goal: to crash stereotypes. At the Lakeshore Foundation, I was in charge of youth programs and the beauty was that I coached kids to live with their disabilities the way I had learned. This was God's hand bringing my life full circle; everything that had been taken away was given back in spades to bless others in my path.

All of the experiences He led me through—getting a normal education, fighting for my place in PE classes, sweating through thousands of hours of rehab, learning to live completely independent, having success in international sport, becoming a homeowner—was for the purpose of teaching what I had learned. Giving back is the way forward for others. God is so good. This is the life He promised to give me when I asked Him from my deathbed to let me live.

As I've spoken across the country, many issues have been brought up as points of discussion to help and offer hope to people with disabilities. Here are some specific lessons I've learned in various areas that can help to *enable* the disabled.

1. Empowering Families

The kids who come to Lakeshore for rehab were easy enough, the parents were often difficult. I could tell how much work I'd have by the way the family entered the gym. A common scenario was the child being pushed in the wheelchair by one or both parents. This was the first thing I zeroed in on and worked to correct.

The person in the chair needs to learn to push his or her own chair. It's like learning to walk. If the kid dropped a pencil and the parent would reach to pick it up, I would have to explain to them to let Timmy figure out how to pick up his own pencil off the floor. This was tough on the parents.

It is important for the family to go through the stages of grief along with the newly disabled because if they do not process these emotions, they can get stuck in one of the stages and place it on the injured family member. The person can't move forward because the family won't let them.

The family is crucial to healing. They must let the person struggle. Some families can't handle this but it is a vital step to independence. If all the members of the family are supporting the person but one is still picking things up off the floor, it will disrupt the rehab. Think about how we teach babies the basics of walking, picking up objects, or getting dressed; we let them struggle. It should be no different when a person is in the position of learning the basics for the second time from a wheelchair or with a prosthetic limb.

I also tell the kids that they are expected to graduate from high school, drive a car, go to college, and live independently; these are the things you are expected to do and need to do. Internal Education Programs (IEPs) often cause conflict between what the state expects from the disabled and what the family and amputee is expecting. In Alabama students are often pigeon-holed into a trade school diploma instead of a regular education. This won't get you into a university. Maybe the state doesn't think they can handle it or won't finish at a university, so let's streamline them all into Plan B, a trade or manual labor. This sets a limited expectation for the kid. The parents are scared into this as well. Maybe junior won't be able to go to a university and succeed in college, so they succumb to the pressure of sending the kid to trade school. *At least they will have something,* they think. This is sabotage. These kids can and should be given a chance and a *choice* in school. We shouldn't be cutting people short, especially those who've already been cut short by life.

Through Lakeshore, I teach kids and families one-on-one the importance of an independent lifestyle, but because of the fame through *Murderball*, I began receiving invitations to speak across the nation at conferences, colleges, major corporations (car manufacturers and airlines interested in proper procedures for interacting with the disabled), local clubs and elementary schools; basically anyone interested in bridging the gap between the abled and disabled communities. Each engagement is an opportunity to educate and change people's perception of the disabled. I am so grateful for the chance I have to help more people.

At a local rehab facility I met a family whose grandpa was disabled. I expressed the need for them to decide as a family to treat Grandpa the same as before. If he was used to getting up in the morning to get the paper on the driveway and then come in to read with a cup of coffee, then they will need to let him do the same thing now; which means, they need to let him struggle for a while as he relearns his routine. The family should not come in and do this for him. If one person in the family usurps his independence then it will sabotage his growth.

The family has a lot to do with the disabled person's ability to move forward, but it's vital for the family to accept their loved one's struggle through the relearning and support his or her independence. They may have guilt or other emotions that make them feel like they have to do everything for the disabled at first, but they need to understand the goal. Family attitudes and behaviors can make or break the mindset of the newly disabled member and can actually make the injury worse if they are not committed to fully transferring as much response-*ability* as possible to counteract the disability.

I once gave a speech in Detroit and a guy came up to me and said his son was in a power chair and "he won't be able to play sports or play baseball or drive a car, and I'm embarrassed around him." I told him he needed to be real careful if he was portraying that, because he is telling his son he is not loved as much now that he can't be productive. I told this father he needed to do something different, like give his son a hug and tell him he loved him no matter what. Father's insecurities will develop in the son and hold him back in life. But if the father believes in his son, the son will believe in himself. It really is as simple as that.

This "life identity" shift is the responsibility of both the disabled person and the family. The family must let go of their hopes and dreams for that member. What was or should have been will now only prevent the newly disabled person from moving forward. Family members must deal with their disappointment, grief, anger and anxious emotions so they will not project them onto the disabled, and truly disable them.

It's a real detriment to everyone to dwell on the loss of abilities and dreams. Likewise, if the father or mother is discouraged when the kid struggles with mundane tasks, or jumps in to help whenever the disabled person struggles, this is a sign the parent is stuck in the past, still grieving what should have been. The person dealing with the amputation or paralysis will have a hard enough time dealing with the trauma and making the shift to a new life. If the family adds their depression to the pot, it is a burden too great to bear for the disabled.

The newly disabled family member must be bolstered and enabled to shift to new hopes and dreams and new abilities. If the family can concentrate on what *is*, the good that is still there, they can move forward together. It starts by realizing that all we have in life is a gift. And a family is a gift that can be empowered as the driving force to accept and make the adjustment to anything life throws their way.

2. Smoothing Transitions

All newly injured people go through a time of transition; physical healing is done with rehab but the mental and emotional healing is done through the stages of grief: shock, denial, pain, anger, depression, acceptance, and hope.

Sometimes it takes a couple of years to get used to your new body and your new life. I can determine where a person is at in their recovery by their attitude and their body language. If they are standoffish, they are most likely still dealing with the reality of the chair. My objective when I encounter these people is to show what is possible. Like people that are addicted to drugs, sometimes a newly disabled needs to hit rock bottom before they are willing to accept a new type of learning and thinking. The mind wants to go back to what was normal. They might have had a bad experience with someone in a chair and they don't want to be like them. A person in transition will focus more on what was taken away, what they don't have, rather than all the possibilities that lay ahead.

So many people give up with their injury, they think life is over. My challenge is to show them what they still have and focus on the future even though they don't always want to hear it. Nobody *wants* to accept being in a chair. But the can do it, just like me. And once they are over the hump, they realize that life is very much a land of opportunity and they will be ready to move forward.

The life they had might be over, but a brand new life is waiting for them in anticipation, ready to surprise them. How great is that?

3. Facilitating Jobs

I was a break-out session speaker at a disability conference in Oregon a few years ago. The purpose was to gather all the disability agencies in Oregon to talk about needs, services, transportation, legislation, parent support groups, durable medical; basically everything A-Z in the disability world was discussed. Andrea Friedman, the actress with Downs Syndrome, was a keynote speaker. She has risen above her disability and is a very influential speaker.

During my session, some of the administrators of the conference brought up the fact that 70% of the 50 million disabled are unemployed. They asked, "How can we change that, Bob?" I told them that employers can look for the person who is approachable, not hiding behind their disability, someone who is confident, secure, college educated. Many employers have the idea that the disabled person will say "you owe me, you have to do this for me, or I will need that special equipment," and the employers don't want to deal with the extra expectations. I believe it is up to the disabled person to adapt to the able-bodied work environment.

Next, the attendees asked about getting turned down for jobs. I said the transition stage is not conducive to presenting yourself in a healthy way during an interview. The confidence of knowing who you are and what you have to offer is the key. I explained how to have a positive interview by making good eye contact with the interviewer, sitting up straight in your chair as much as you are able (exercise helps this), and taking the initiative to sell yourself. I also told them my personal experience.

When I first started looking for jobs after graduate school, I wasn't hired because I was overqualified. I had a graduate degree, I had worked at the Paralympics in Atlanta, but then I was out of work and needed to pay my bills. I wanted to be independent so I took anything I could to keep the cash flowing while I found a career. It is much better to walk into a company with any kind of job, even one that is beneath you, than to have a six-month vacancy on your resume. I worked at a pizza place taking orders over the phone, I worked in sales, and I worked a switchboard; whatever it took to stay afloat. I looked for an employment agency specifically for the disabled. There wasn't one. But, there are many employment agencies in every city. Why do we want it curtailed to us? Why do I want mainstream to curtail to me because I am disabled? I need to adapt to mainstream as much as possible; it's up to me to fit in and not expect to be catered to because I am special.

An employer can ask how I lost my limbs but they cannot legally ask if I can pick up a phone or type or perform the job. They look at me and think, obviously he can't type, obviously he can't answer the phone, but this is discrimination. They are so caught up in my appearance that they forget the obvious: I would not be there applying if I couldn't handle it; that would be silly. So it's up to me to fill in the gap, to answer the questions they can't legally ask. I say, "the traffic was thick," or "As I was typing my resume..." I pull something out of my wallet or put my phone on vibrate to give them a visual of what I can do.

It's up to the disabled to turn the experience into a positive one. If you are insecure and hiding behind your chair, an employer will not have a favorable opinion of you. Extend your hand. It is up to you to make the person comfortable or they won't hire you. You have to go the extra mile.

Something that really helps in landing a job is exercise and playing sports because as a disabled person, we are already behind the 8-ball in the interview. Employers do not want to hire you just by looking at you; they assume you are needy. So if you have sports on your resume, they get the impression you are healthy, you are less susceptible to getting sick, you will be taking less time off, etc. In other words, *they won't have to take care of you.*

Finally, I took the liberty to say that I couldn't help but notice some of the attendees made a few trips to the buffet. As disabled people, we need to watch that, eat only half the dessert. It matters.

I try to make it personal to my audience by calling them out. Healthy living is something we can do to get the job, to make ourselves more approachable. The way you think is the way you act. And diet and exercise is an important way to show you know how to handle yourself and do what's good for everyone.

4. Engaging the Public

The best classroom to break stereotypes will always be out in public: especially restaurants, airplanes, and stores.

One of the hard things for able-bodied people to understand is that we don't want people to jump in and help us when we struggle, unless we ask for help. I speak for those I know are of the same mindset here. I purposely do not have handles on the back of my chair because I do not want people pushing me. I can roll myself. If I am out at the grocery store, then I am able to buy groceries and put them in my car unassisted. If I need an item from a higher shelf that I can't reach, I will ask for help. But don't jump in and think you need to save me. Don't assume that I came out in public without being able to handle it.

At first, people are never quite sure how to respond to me. When I enter a restaurant, the hostess is not sure where to seat me, the waiter doesn't know how to serve me, the patrons can't stop staring. Generally, everywhere I go in public there is confusion on the faces

I encounter; they're not sure if they should help me or let me be. But they always stare.

I'm used to people staring at me. It's up to me to make them feel comfortable, to be polite, and show them that I can handle whatever situation I'm currently in. And it's up to the person I'm encountering to take my cues. A reporter once said to me that he wasn't sure if he should shake my arm because he thought he might hurt me. If I volunteer to reach out and shake hands with you, then it must mean I'm not afraid of hurting myself with a handshake. I wouldn't choose to put myself in a painful position. Not to mention that my surgery was 35 years ago. I'm pretty sure the incisions have healed by now. *Wanting* to shake hands with me is a different issue entirely. Granted, it won't be a "normal" handshake; I don't have fingers. But when I offer my stump, it's to show respect and that I am happy to meet you. It's up to you to take it, just like you would a hand.

This is what I try to demonstrate and "teach" in every encounter, every day.

5. Improving Air Travel

I fly all over the country for team tournaments, for speaking engagements, for vacation, to go see my family, etc. Anytime I fly into a big city, there are plenty of amenities for the disabled so it makes it easier. Smaller cities with smaller airports are a little harder to navigate. It usually means you have to go outside to board the plane. If there is a ramp, and it's not raining, I will scoot up the ramp or climb the stairs and the airline employee will carry my chair to the cargo hold underneath the plane. Most airlines also have lifts that raise a platform to the door.

I get a lot of looks scooting down the aisle of the plane because I'm about the same height as the armrest.

The key to flying is to be early. All airlines are great at boarding the disabled early so as not to disrupt the other passengers. If I arrive late, it can be a huge issue; the passengers are cranky, the customer service is terrible and we all have a very bad experience. It is up to me to arrive early, to go to the desk at the gate right away and ask the attendant what time they want me to be available to board the plane; and I say "perfect, I'll be here." It's up to me to be proactive and take care of myself. It is up to the airlines to have a system, to know how to board the disabled early, so we are not in the way and holding up the boarding process.

Our rugby team has flown several times together on our way to out-of-state tournaments. Once, when the flight attendant brought drinks, my cup of Coke came with a lid and a straw. I didn't ask for a lid or a straw. My teammate, Willard, who probably should have had a lid on his drink, didn't get a lid. Apparently I wouldn't be able to handle my drink without spilling it. Willard, who has arms, hands, and fingers, must have seemed he could handle a drink without a lid.

"Nice kids' cup, Lujano," Willard said.

But I got the last laugh because Willard spilled his drink while he was harassing me! Coke and ice cubes everywhere! I offered him my kids' cup.

We joke around but the point is, people will decide what we can and can't handle based on our appearance. It's frustrating, but it's reality.

I once flew through Chicago and my plane was late coming in. It was chaos. Everyone was hungry, including me, and there were a million people in line at the restaurant near the gate. There was a shorter time between the connecting flights so the stress level of most people was high. I always carry my luggage on my lap so I don't have to deal with baggage claim, but this was an extra burden in dealing with the stressed out crowd and needing to eat. I needed to take initiative despite the many hurdles.

My food choice between flights was going to be based on what little I could carry. I can carry a tray using my mouth and one arm and wheel with the other arm, but, this place was crowded and I had a large duffel bag on my lap. I definitely want to try first to see what I can do and if I need help I will ask, no problem. Most people will ask if I need assistance and some did; I'm fine being asked. But in the end I decided not to make the situation worse and chose small items I could handle, then moved out of the way in that busy place.

In that situation, as in many such airport challenges, it's important to do what you can to take care of yourself. Even foregoing your preferred food, method or route. Be accommodating and gracious, and people will want to be accommodating and gracious to you.

6. Navigating Stores and Restaurants

My teammate Andy Cohn tells a story in *Murderball* that he was putting groceries into the back of his car and someone asked if he needed them to load the groceries for him. He said what I said above, that if he couldn't handle putting groceries in his car by himself, he would have brought someone with him or wouldn't have come at all. A disabled person is not going to put themselves into a situation they can't handle. That would be embarrassing, not to mention the level of vulnerability it would take to go to a place and then sit there and wait for help.

The able-bodied feel guilty if they see a person struggle and don't offer assistance. But if the able-bodied person offers assistance, they might offend the disabled person who is doing their best to be independent. The offense, or discrimination, is in the person's expressed doubt; the immediate dismissal of the person and their abilities. If you jump in and help the person without asking, you are usurping their independence. If you look at someone and think, *they can't do this*, that's discrimination. It is not up to you to decide what that person can or cannot do, and it is not up to you to jump in and take over.

If it appears a disabled person truly needs help, just ask if you can assist in any way and wait. Many disabled people are rude because they're having a bad day, or maybe you are the thousandth person that day to ask the same question. But don't let this stop you from being friendly.

Most disabled people are happy to be independent and happy to receive help when they need it.

One time I was at a mall and a man saw me rolling toward the door so he ran back and said 'Hey, I'm coming, hold up!' He made a really big scene of opening the door for me and I was really embarrassed. He meant well, but it drew attention to me and made me feel *disabled*.

Had I been someone else, I might have said, "Believe it or not, I can open these big heavy glass doors at the mall. I don't need to reach for the button so the door will open by itself. I can open any door in front of me." But instead I said thank you and rolled away.

At Costco, I was pushing my cart and there was a family that decided I needed help. The dad *told* the son to come over and push my cart for me out to my car, which the son promptly did. They were Hispanic so I gave them extra grace and we bonded right away. The dad wrote his phone number on a piece of paper and gave it to me! He told me that anytime I needed help, to call him and he would have his son come to push my cart for me because it would be good for his son. *Good for his son?* The father wanted to give the son something to do, educate him to appreciate what he had.

I don't mean to sound like a jerk, but give me a break. Disabled people are not in a chair to help kids learn to serve or so someone can feel better about themselves. Would he volunteer to assign his son's services to an able-bodied person? I wanted to say, "Okay, sir, if this is what you think I need!" But I just have to laugh it off.

It was nice of him to offer his son to help me around town. I don't look down on him because I know he meant well. But it wasn't a kindness to jump in and assume I needed something I didn't ask for. If I wasn't able to handle Costco, I wouldn't go. Do able-bodied people voluntarily put themselves into situations they know they can't handle? Who wants that kind of attention? We already stick out as "abnormal" by being in a wheelchair; we can't really blend in anywhere, so there's no way I would put myself in a situation I couldn't handle just to get attention and appear needy.

Kids are taught not to stare or ask questions, so when a parent makes a big deal about the kid's behavior in any public place, I usually make a bee-line to them and start talking. I can change the situation by making the first move. This happened once at a fast food place.

I was sitting near the play area eating my food and a little boy on the play equipment kept staring at me. The mom kept saying, "Jimmy, keep playing." The kid would start playing again and then soon stop to watch me eat again. Finally, his food came but he stared at me instead of eating. So I went over to them, I asked the mom for permission to talk to him, but Jimmy was suddenly shy so I talked to the mom. Like most people, she was really glad I came over to break the awkward silence. I simply tried to make them comfortable.

When I speak to elementary students, I teach them how to approach a disabled person. They may have had someone in their family that needed a lot of attention, so their impression is that all disabled need a personal care assistant. I ask them to name the different types of physical disabilities and then I talk about seeing someone in public. It's okay to ask questions, shake their hand; there's no guarantee you will get a positive answer but you can say, "Hi, my name is Billy, what do you like to do? And by the way, what happened?"

Some people see handles on the back of a wheelchair and think its okay to start pushing the person all over the place; this is actually rude. There is nothing wrong with asking, but you wouldn't treat an able-bodied person like a child and move them to another part of the room without their permission. So when in doubt, ask, and offer respect whatever the situation.

I love to teach the disabled community to grab ahold of an independent lifestyle. And I love to speak to the able-bodied to teach them how to treat the disabled. I love to speak to families who are currently going through the tragedy of a new disability to show them that life isn't over. Teaching by example, crashing stereotypes, is my passion. It is the life I have been given. And I am so blessed.

"You did not choose me, but I chose you and appointed you so that you might go and bear fruit [love, joy, peace, patience, kindness, goodness, gentleness, faithfulness, and self-control]."

John 15:16 & Galatians 5:22 NIV

17

Thank God I'm Able

I WENT INTO SURGERY AS BOB and I came out as Bob. Nothing changed inside of me. My path in life, however, was forever changed for the better.

How great it is to have a disability. Everything in life is a mindset. Mine was pretty clear-cut; I wanted to be an athlete. The Lord said to me, "Okay, you are going to play sports but it's going to be different than you imagine." I'm not playing baseball on TV like I had hoped, but I was able to represent my country in a full-contact sport. I am still highly competitive. My spirit or purpose was not taken away from me in the operating room; it was given to me. God did not take away my original passion for sports and replace it with something else. What He said over me in that surgical room was, "The world already has a Pete Rose, that part is covered. I need you to affect the world *this way*. Yes, Bob, you will still have your dream but it will be *this way*." I am so grateful.

Everything in my life is permeated by my faith in God. Back in 1979 I could not see a purpose for my life; I only knew that I wanted to live and that I wanted to follow Jesus. Little by little, God through his grace showed me my purpose as he guided me through life's trials and accomplishments.

I read *Purpose-Driven Life* by Rick Warren when it first came out and to me, the whole synopsis of that book is to have a relationship with God through Jesus and to use your life to serve God and serve people. This is the ultimate purpose of everyone; love God and love people no matter what condition you are in. Whether you are the janitor, or Bill Gates, or a surgeon who saves kids' lives, or somewhere in between, we all serve each other, we all have a purpose in God's plan. The Lord did not cause my illness, but I will always believe that he intended to use it for the benefit of others. I believe He had a role and a function for me to play in His will.

My life has not been easy. It hurt to be abused by my dad and grandpa and it hurt that my mom left. But I am so grateful that I had a dad who was there and who stood up for me when I needed it.

Some people mistake my attitude as something that is not believable or achievable. It is a daily choice. Bitterness and joy cannot inhabit the same space at the same time. I choose joy. I've always wanted to live life to the fullest. No matter how painful or how difficult some events or time periods have been, I have never regretted my decision to choose life and I have never contemplated suicide. A boy once asked me after I spoke if I would change my life if I could. I said no; I don't think my life would have turned out as great as it has. In hindsight, maybe this saved me from the pattern of abuse. Maybe it started a legacy of love.

Losing my limbs was the best thing that ever happened to me. Look at what I would have missed! I have travelled the world, played on the international stage and I get to work at Lakeshore.

When Jesus asked me if I wanted to go home or live, and I told Him I wanted to live, I knew that He would always be there with me my whole life to help me and provide for me. That's "who" He is. He doesn't call us to Him and then leave us hanging out to dry. He honors our decision by having our backs; He is our creator, our protector, our provider, and our security. He is just, merciful, graceful, loving, and forgiving. He is the sovereign Lord of the universe. Who He is is who He wants us to be to each other.

I am disappointed that I have failed Him many times during my life in my thoughts and actions. I have made some bad decisions and behaved in ways I am not proud of. Besides the activities I've already mentioned, sometimes I am still conscious about the way people think about me or view me. This is sinful because even though I know who

I am in Christ, I still struggle with being a people-pleaser. I still have insecurities.

When I meet someone for the first time, I feel like I need that person to look beyond the chair and the scars and get them to accept me. In my mind I think, "What do I have to do to get them to like me?" Often, if I don't accomplish this, I feel like I have failed. I messed up by not approaching the person in the right way. I always ask myself, "Was it me or my lack of limbs?"

As a person with a disability, I need to come across as approachable. I don't want them to be turned off by me because they are afraid of my appearance. I want people to approach me and like me. I'm hurt if they don't, but that's life and God still wants me to reach out and show love.

I feel it is my job to educate people but sometimes it happens when I don't expect it or it's at inopportune times. I was on a date recently and a five-year-old girl came up and asked, "What happened?" I didn't mind, and I told her to keep asking questions but her parents kept apologizing. I told them not to discourage her; it's good to learn by asking questions. My date was gracious but she didn't say much about the little girl's questions.

I can usually tell within the first twenty minutes whether or not a woman is receptive to the idea of dating me. I can read the questions in her mind as we talk. "Could we have children? Could I handle the disability? Could I bear to be seen with him in public?" The fact that this woman was out with me was a good sign, but I wasn't sure if the little girl's questions had changed her mind about what she could handle longer term.

Since Ruby, I've had some rocky relationships. On the one hand, I'm having the opposite problem I used to have. There are women who throw themselves at disabled men specifically *because* they're disabled. I've had my fair share of offers and these bold women are difficult to ward off. I want to be loved like everyone else. The temptation is strong, but I resist because I know these are not godly women. This is not the type of relationship that would honor God.

On the other hand, I was engaged to a woman named *Maria. I met her back in the fall of 1988 at the University of Dallas. I was taking theology and religious studies classes with the intent of becoming a priest. We befriended right away; she is intelligent, kind, genuine, selfless, has a joyful spirit, and was a real breath of fresh air. We went to dinner and watched movies at her house, but it was all innocent because I seriously thought I was headed to the priesthood. We hung out for a year-and-a-half until I switched schools. We kept in touch until 1996 and then we lost contact.

After *Murderball* came out, I had dinner with a mutual friend and inquired about her. The friend said she was still single so I gave him my business card to forward to her. A few years went by and we finally connected. The friendship was rekindled; we started a long-distance relationship and took turns flying back and forth from Houston where she was to Birmingham where I was. After two years it was getting serious so I proposed. We set a wedding date for September of 2011. A few months before the wedding, she started having some issues and began to pull away. We also hadn't settled where we would live. One of us would have to move and neither of us wanted to. It was best to end it.

I'm sad that we don't talk anymore because she is an outstanding woman and I have a lot of respect for her. I'm grateful to have been engaged, to be able to say I was. The old adage is true: it's better to have loved and lost than never to have loved at all. Love is from God. It's the greatest gift to receive love; it's a virtue to have and to give. It was painful to lose her love because I know that it was real and true. I was truly loved. That's what is great; you know you have loved and been loved because it aches when it's gone.

It's a beautiful ache because I know that I really experienced it. I am so thankful for that ache. I was truly loved. It is the grace of God that allows endurance. I'm sad but I'm thankful for the experience and it is a testament that God knows what is best for our lives and I thank Him for that.

In April, 2012, I was promoted at Lakeshore Foundation from Recreation Specialist to Information Specialist through the National Center of Health Promotions Physical Activity and Disability (NCHPAD) as part of the University of Alabama at Birmingham/ Lakeshore Foundation Research Collaborative. That's a mouthful that basically means that the NCHPAD, through Lakeshore, is positioning itself to be a national resource center for people with physical disabilities. There is an 800 number and I might get a call from someone in Ohio who broke their wheelchair and they need to know who to contact; or I might get someone in Hawaii who needs an in-home physical therapist. The national database being compiled puts these callers in touch with resources in their local area. I also travel a lot for training and development and this gives me a chance to personally meet those in the disabled communities across the nation. We are always about diet and exercise and promoting a holistic mindset to live life with a healthy mind, body, and spirit. Any resource that can point the disabled in that direction is a win for everyone.

A gift God gave to me is the privilege of bringing communion to the elderly at the Senior Center. I get to do a mini mass, say prayers, give a short homily and give communion. It's similar to what a priest does, although not exactly. God is so good in His redemption plan in our lives. I see this as His way of answering my early desire to become a priest. I am so thankful for this.

Around this time, my great nephew (Lisa's grandson), Anthony David Oliver, died. He was born with half a heart so we knew he wouldn't live long. Being an eternal optimist, I thought he would survive for many years. He was shy at first but once he warmed up to you he was joyful and playful. The last time I saw him was in February of 2012. I was in Houston for a rugby tournament and my dad and Lisa came with Ado (as we called him) and Ado's parents, Josh and Erica, to see me play. When they arrived, I rolled down the long corridor to meet them in their hotel room. Ado was so excited that he ran down the hall and jumped in my lap to greet me! He was so full of love as he gave me a warm hug. He told me he loved me.

He had more love in a half a heart than some of us will ever have.

That moment pierced my memory in August of that year when I got the call that he had passed. I was in Atlanta giving a lecture and was aware he had been hospitalized a week earlier. When my dad called me to give me the news, he broke down and cried, and so did I. It reminded me of when we cried together in my hospital bed. The older members of our family were right back to that earlier time too, a fatal illness threatening to take a child's life; only this time it actually was fatal.

I called Josh to offer my condolences but I didn't know what to say to him. I have no experience with children dying. I told him the only thing I knew to be true: Ado was with the Lord, he's no longer suffering, and we will see him again. I really thought he would survive because I had. I don't understand it, but God knows what He's doing.

Josh and Erica were told to abort Ado in utero. His tiny half heart was visible on the imaging screen. They chose life. Because of this, we were able to experience God's love and joy for 3 ½ years through Ado. We would have missed out on so many blessings if she had killed him. We would have missed the joy.

It rained during his funeral. Erica eulogized him and was a pallbearer, even helping to lower him into the ground. I asked her why she did this. She told me that she would never be able to give him another birthday party, another tribute, or be able to toast his achievements. This was her way of celebrating him one final time. She showed great strength and courage.

At the graveside there was a single thunderclap. Ado had never failed to remind us that thunder was Jesus jumping up and down in heaven.

Uncle Richard died on November 26, 2013. I, along with the rest of my family thought we would never see the day. This man exhibited so many life giving qualities that no one saw it coming. My Uncle will have a permanent fixture in my childhood since he was the one who not only was there to bring laughter and joy during tough times but he was also the one to take me to the hospital when my life was about to change. He seemed to always be around to help when a family member or a stranger was in need.

I will remember the things people said about him at his funeral. He was the man who got involved in church and community events. I remember asking him why he did this and his response was "I do not want our Mexican people to look bad." He made us feel proud to be Mexican. He was the one that took me to Mexico when I was 11 years old. He was the one who went with me, to then Yugoslavia, on a pilgrimage journey. He was the one who was just a fanatic when it came to rooting for his hometown team. All Kansas teams were his favorite, especially the Wichita State Shockers, the KC Chiefs, the KC Royals and the Kansas Jayhawks.

Uncle Richard was also a very proud family man. Although he did not have any kids of his own, he was Godfather to many of his nieces and nephews. He was always introducing me to relatives that I did not know existed. He could tell you how we were related. He was very instrumental in introducing me to family in Hutchinson, Kansas, in Chicago, Illinois, and in San Jose, California. To this very day I keep tabs on family that live in those areas and look forward to seeing them. He was also the man who took it upon himself to take care of my grandmother Hope, his mother, when she started to lose her independence. He went above and beyond.

In Mexican culture, a Nino, holds a special place in a family similar to a Godfather. It is very sacred. Richard was this person. He told us to embrace our Catholic faith and serve a role in the church. This was something he led by example. My Dad gave Richard the nick-name "Boss-man." He was that 1000 times over. You either loved him for it or had issue with it. I could not imagine anyone else filling that role. I had to struggle to learn to love it, but I did as best I could. IIis death marked only the third time I saw my Dad cry.

I COULD EASILY HAVE DIED at any point during my illness. But that wasn't the plan. That wasn't what God had for me. Not everyone is comfortable with their disability. I am fortunate that God kept me alive. All the good I have is from my faith in Him. Not everyone has my faith; but look for it. It can do so much for you, it can take you places you never thought possible, you will do things far greater than you thought you could accomplish, you will have opportunities you wouldn't have had otherwise. Maybe you have a vision of being rich and successful. Rich and successful to me is that I have a roof over my head, I have a job that provides for my house, pays my bills, my car, and I don't need a caregiver. I am very blessed.

My disability is normal to me (whatever normal means) because this is how I have lived the majority of my life. I see myself as able. My objective in life is to meet life head on and not sit back and let it pass by. Whatever I'm given, whatever condition I am in, I will praise God for my life, I will love everybody and give thanks and praise that I am healthy, active, physically fit, and I can honor my body as a temple of the Lord.

I want to have a serious daily relationship with Christ, not just for an hour on Sunday. I want to give thanks no matter how difficult life gets. If I left God, where would I go? Nowhere else offers eternal peace, starting in the here-and-now. Even if I was dirt poor financially, I would be rich because I have Jesus. If I was filthy rich financially, but did not have Jesus, I would have nothing. Jesus is life. This is who I am and I thank the Lord for that.

Able: "Having necessary power, skill, resources, or qualifications."

—Dictionary.com

God is able.

"I'm not saying that I have this all together, that I have it made. But I am well on my way, reaching out for Christ, who has so wondrously reached out for me. Friends, don't get me wrong: By no means do I count myself an expert in all of this, but I've got my eye on the goal, where God is beckoning us onward—to Jesus. I'm off and running and I'm not turning back."

Philippians 3:12-14 MSG

Bob's Acknowledgements

FIRST AND FOREMOST I HAVE to thank God for creating me to be in his service. I am so thankful to have my disability for it has allowed me to have such a blessed life. It has made me realize how much I depend on his grace, love, and mercy. I am so thankful that he has directed me to places I have never been, to people I've never met and to be part of social changes that have shaped our culture and world.

Scripture says in Matthew 6:25-34 in summary, how God provides for the lilies of the field and that he will provide for you as well.

God has provided by giving me such a loving, supportive and caring family. Yet, stern enough to let me go and let me be what God has created. I am so thankful for all the Lujano family members and those related to the Lujano family.

A Special thank you and I love you for my Grandmother Hope (Esperanza). I know her love and prayers have been the spiritual force that has helped in guiding my own faith journey.

A special thank you to my Dad, Bob Sr. He has taught me how to be a man. I am so thankful that you have been the instrument God used to provide for me. I don't know where I would be without you. Thank you for being a living example of the importance of education. Thank you for all the discipline and love. All I ever wanted to do was make you proud.

A big thank you and I love you to my sister Lisa who has been my best friend for so many years. You have always been that example of strength under fire. You are also living proof that God provides. You set the example of never being afraid. You are so much like Dad in being strong, smart and caring. You have always been my biggest fan and I always have and will always be yours.

To John, Paul, and Willie, Thank you for being my all-time favorite sports heroes. My childhood memories are filled with so many struggles, joys, sadness and laughter. I am so thankful to go through all that with you. My childhood memories always include you.

To Edna, who is my mother and has been the most difficult person that I have ever loved. Thank you for loving me and for being that person who has my back. Thank you for the love of the Carpenter and De La Garza families. Nanny and Popo are always in my prayers.

Uncle Richard, Aunt Mary, Uncle Louis, Tio Gonzalo, Little Mary, Felipe Lujano, Danny Martinez, the whole Mora family, Aunt Marcelina, Gloria, Marie and Dave, I have so many wonderful memories and so much love for who you are and all that you've done for me. Never will I forget.

This book was specially written to thank God and to show the next generation of Lujano family members that if you put your faith in God and educate your mind, you can go places never imagined. So, for my brothers Joe and Julian, my nephews Josh and Brent, may God bless you tenfold even more than he has blessed me. May he bless your families, especially Anthony, Mia, Isaiah, Will, Elijah, RJ, AJ, Hannah and Johnny.

A special thank you goes to my childhood best friend, Raymond John Arellano. Your friendship while I lived with Grandma Hope helped me get through the difficult times. I am especially grateful that you came to visit me in the hospital. I will never forget that kindness.

Thank you for my friends for life for being there when things seem bleak and for looking to put a smile on my face: John Hennessey, The Ander's family, the Carter-Boff family, the Ibanez family, the Montee family, the Zwitt family, the Haynes family, the Carboni family, the Bruder family, the Pate family, the Price family, the Orr family, Ken and Joy CarterBoff, and the Bachman family.

I cannot forget all the love from my work family, the Lakeshore Foundation, NCHPAD family, and the Demolition family. Our best is still ahead, thank for allowing me to be part of it. It has been my honor to be part of this family.

I also want to include all the churches and parishes that have been instrumental in my faith development: Prince of Peace, Our Lady of Sorrow, Briarwood Church, my BSF brothers, in Birmingham, Alabama, St. Michael in Grand Prairie, Texas, and Our Lady of Guadalupe in Newton, Kansas. Thank you to all the Popes, Bishops, Priests, and lay workers, that have been so instrumental in challenging me to improving my relationship with God. Always a beautiful struggle!

A BIG thank you to everyone that has written me letters, made phone calls, and sent emails of love, prayers and support; I love you and I know you have been with me all this time. You will always be in my heart.

I would like to extend a special thank you to Roger Stauback, Julius Erving, and Tony Hill for calling me, for sending messages, and for visiting me in the hospital. I will always treasure this kindness from my heroes when I thought my sports days were over.

Last but not least a big special Thank you to my friend for life Tara Schiro and her beautiful family of Tiffany, Vince, and husband Frank. Your love, dedication and support of me have made this book possible. May God continue to bless your lives and all of your endeavors. Tara, I said from the beginning we would need to be patient and we have, thanks be to God.

–Bob Lujano

"Are you tired? Worn out? Burned out on religion? Come to me. Get away with me and you'll recover your life. I'll show you how to take a real rest. Walk with me and work with me—watch how I do it. Learn the unforced rhythms of grace. I won't lay anything heavy or ill-fitting on you. Keep company with me and you'll learn to live freely and lightly."

Matthew 11:28-30 MSG

Tara's Acknowledgments

THE FIRST PERSON I NEED to thank is Lisa Lujano. She rushed over to me during a Women's Entrepreneur luncheon after hearing my 30 second elevator speech. *You're a writer? My brother has a story! Will you write his story?* I still remember the smile on your face, how you gushed when you spoke of him. How could I say no? Your example of loyalty and compassion is contagious. Thank you for being your brother's cheerleader and for inviting me into your spirit squad.

A big thank you goes to the entire Lujano family for your patience during this process. The questions were sometimes redundant and not always easy to answer. The emotions 36 years later are still painful and I am deeply grateful for your honesty, your transparency, your vulnerability and your willingness to participate. Despite the dysfunction, the love you have for each other and the spirit to fight and keep moving forward is admirable. It was a joy to get to know you. You will be forever in my heart and always in my circle of friends.

Thank you, Dr. Rennebohm, for your willingness to speak to me and for your transparency. You are a Super Hero in this story. The comment I heard repeatedly from the Lujano family was how grateful they are for you and for your determination to save Bob's life. You may have questioned your efforts against a deadly disease, but your commitment to his care paid worldwide dividends; Bob impacts everyone he meets. Thank you for your dedication and service in the medical field. Your contributions have eternal value.

Thank you to my man, my best friend and husband, Frank. This project was a long, emotional road and I am so grateful that you didn't give up on me. You helped me verbally process, you gave me space to brood, and you pushed me to the finish line. Thank you for loving me just the way I am and for telling me I am perfect for you. Even when I'm not. Love you back. Forever yours.

Thank you to my two favorite kids on the planet, Tiffany and Vince, for putting up with piles of laundry and an empty refrigerator during the final stages of publication. Well, ok, let's be honest; domesticity is not a part of my DNA so thank you for learning how to order food. You are my heroes, so witty and smart and capable in every way. Your belief in me and the excitement in your eyes propel me forward. I love you as high as heaven and back. However, I am the only true Ninja in the house.

Thank you to Doug and Kathy Whittle, the first people to believe in me as a writer and for telling me that I could. The leg lamp is coming under separate cover.

Mick Silva. I seriously do not know what I would do without you as my editor and friend. You patiently listened to my rants and guided my writing with more compassion and grace I have ever experienced. This book, my writing, would not be what it is without you. Thank you for your dedication and passion to those of us you coach and for always believing we can. See you in the next book.

Thank you to Cary Norton (www.CaryNorton.com) for Bob's cover photo; to Jill Anders for Bob's author photo; to Nicole Pollard Photography for Tara's author photo; to Lena Giron for stepping in at the last minute to proofread and wipe my tears; to Glendon at Streetlight Graphics for being so patient with me in my slightly panicked state and for doing fabulous work on the formatting and cover design.

Thank you to all the friends and relatives who cheered from afar as I completed mile after mile of this marathon. The Heath High School alumni, the Heath Church of Christ friends, the 34th street gang, the Riffell family, the Village family; your pom-poms were felt and it made a difference.

A special thank you to Michael Roberts and Tom Foster; you make me laugh, plain and simple. On the days I thought the creativity was nowhere in sight, you always had something witty in your pocket that made me feel like I could, too (write something witty or profound). Michael, *Charmland* is next.

To "the crew" in holding: Steve N., Tina, Pam, Kevin, Carl, Carlton, Freida, Lena, Sara, Casey, Chill, Gordan, John, Mary Beth, Svetlana, Manny, Jack, and the many faces we see on a regular basis: thanks for sharing the dream with me. You are a pleasure to know and cross with. I predict one of us will invent an app for easily locating the nearest outlet. Remember to be real in your pantomime.

Miss Kolmar, wherever you are, my fourth and fifth grade teacher at Cherry Valley Elementary. You saw a flicker of flame in my soul and I'm forever grateful that I could see it reflected in your eyes. I've never forgotten that revealing look, "that girl has something special." Your silent belief in me is something I've referred to many times when doubt threatens to take over. Thank you for seeing what I couldn't and for showing me that I can.

A very large thank you to Bob Lujano. You are the most beautiful person I know. I've agonized for seven long years to do your story justice, to create a legacy that you will be proud to share. You were patient with me when I didn't deserve it. You were gracious when I was rude. You loved when I did not believe I could do this. You were kind when I talked too much. You trusted me with your story when you probably shouldn't have. Your trust and faith in God is what got us here. I am so thankful and grateful for all you have modeled. I have learned so much from you.

Thank you to the Triune God, the Father, Son, and Holy Spirit. I'm so grateful for your protection, provision, and security; you are faithful, trustworthy, unwavering, healer, redeemer, transformer, giver of all things, and the very breath in my lungs. You never left me as I agonized over your words, deliberated over structure and theme, and sat frozen in front of the keyboard hoping for inspiration. Thank you for showing your love and purpose for us, and thank you for inviting me to document Bob's story within Your story. I hope it makes you proud.

–Tara Schiro

"Why would you ever complain, or whine, saying 'God has lost track of me. He doesn't care what happens to me?' Don't you know anything? Haven't you been listening? God doesn't come and go. God lasts. He's creator of all you can see or imagine. He doesn't get tired out, doesn't pause to catch his breath. And he knows everything, inside and out. He energizes those who get tired. But those who wait upon God get fresh strength. They spread their wings and soar like eagles, they run and don't get tired, they walk and don't lag behind."

Isaiah 40:28-31 MSG

Resources

www.NoArmsNoLegsNoProblem.com

Bob Lujano
www.BobLujano.com
Information Specialist, NCHPAD at Lakeshore Foundation
4000 Ridgeway Drive
Birmingham, Alabama – 35209
Toll-Free 1-800-900-8086

Tara Schiro
www.TaraSchiro.com

Lakeshore Foundation
Recreation, Rehabilitation, Research, and Official Training Site for
the U.S. Olympic and Paralympic Athletes
www.lakeshore.org
4000 Ridgeway Drive
Birmingham, AL 35209
205-313-7400
information@lakeshore.org
https://www.facebook.com/lakeshorefoundation
https://twitter.com/LakeshoreFound

**Lima Foxtrot at Lakeshore Foundation for Recently Wounded
Veterans**
4000 Ridgeway Drive
Birmingham, AL 35209

205-313-7400
information@lakeshore.org
National Center on Health, Physical Activity and Disability (NCHPAD)
4000 Ridgeway Drive
Birmingham, Alabama – 35209
Toll-Free 1-800-900-8086
www.nchpad.org
email@nchpad.org
https://www.facebook.com/nchpad
https://twitter.com/NCHPAD

United States Quad Rugby Association
www.quadrugby.com
https://www.facebook.com/USQRAQuadRugby
https://twitter.com/USQRA

Disabled Sports USA
451 Hungerford Drive, Suite 100
Rockville, Maryland 20850
www.disabledsportsusa.org

New Life Ministries
Every Man's Battle, Lose it for Life, Healing is a Choice, Women in the Battle, Marriage Solution Workshop, New Life TV, New Life Live!
www.NewLife.com
www.tv.newlife.com

Saddleback Church
www.Saddleback.com

Real Life Church
www.RealLifeChurch.org

KKLA Radio

www.kkla.com

Focus on the Family
www.FocusontheFamily.com

Bible Study Fellowship
Bible classes. For every age. Around the world.
www.BSFInternational.org

Children of the Nations
Raising Children Who Transform Nations
Sponsor a child for $32/month in the Dominican Republic, Haiti, Liberia, Malawi, Sierra Leone, or Uganda
www.COTNI.org

ON JANUARY 7, 1979, BOB Lujano contracted meningococcemia, a rare form of meningitis. To save his life, all four limbs had to be amputated. From that day on, Lujano's goal has been to live an independent life like everyone else. He earned his master's degree in Recreation/Sports Management from the University of Tennessee, won a bronze medal at the 2004 Paralympic Games in Athens, Greece, co-starred in the Academy nominated documentary "Murderball" and was a guest on Larry King Live. Lujano continues to work at the Lakeshore Foundation, an official U.S. Olympic and Paralympic training site as well as home to the Lima Foxtrot program for recently wounded veterans. Lujano is an Information Specialist for NCHPAD, the National Center on Health, Physical Activity, and Disability. He is an advocate in the area of adaptive and competitive wheelchair sports and serves as President for the USQRA, the United States Quad Rugby Association. In 2013 he was listed as one of the 20 Most Beautiful People in Birmingham, Alabama. Lujano is a motivational speaker, resides in Birmingham, Alabama, and lives a completely independent lifestyle. www.BobLujano.com